Shipwreck Treasures, Incan Gold, and Living on Ice

Celebrating 50 Years of Adventure

Ed Sobey, PhD

Acknowledgements

Thanks first and foremost to my wife, Barbara, for encouraging me, helping me, and joining me on so many adventures. Many of these adventures would not have occurred without her support or participation.

Likewise I thank and apologize to our sons Woody and Andrew. I thank them for being eager participants in many of our adventure and apologize for exposing them to so many iffy situations. Paddling to Assateague Island when wind and waves had thwarted the attempt by buff college students. Climbing rocks with minimal instruction. SCUBA diving with me. These experiences could have turned them away from nature and adventure, but it brought them closer. For that I am delighted.

Thanks to Jean and John Weigant for their partnership in several adventures sailing, kayaking, and hiking, and for their editing of this manuscript. Jean did an exceptional job catching the myriad errors I made. Frank Handler also provided edits. Frank and I worked together to revive and run the Pacific Northwest Chapter of The Explorers Club for a decade. Steve McCracken and Pete Marshall, running friends, reviewed the drafts. Thank you.

Thanks to all the other people I shared a night or two in a tent, aboard a boat, or in a hut in Antarctica.

It's been a grand ride and I can only hope it's not over.

Ed

Shipwreck Treasures, Incan Gold, and

Living on Ice

Celebrating 50 Years of Adventure

Across the oceans

Sweetwater Paddling

Now On exhibit

Traveling on a Paper Rocket

Short Hike

Parting Thought

Appendix

Across oceans

With a one-year deferment from the Navy I went to graduate school in oceanography at Oregon State University in the fall 1969. There Barbara and I met and I went on my first research expedition.

Hang on Tightly and Look Up

The aft deck of the RV Cayuse was rocking wildly and was awash in sea water. I was desperately trying to hold on and not be carried overboard. Big waves were breaking over the stern and a heavy rain pelted us from above. "So this is oceanography?" I wondered.

My first research cruise in 1969 was a wild ride and grand adventure. It was grand in that I learned a lot and no one got killed.

We sailed from Newport, Oregon and the smell of the diesel engine imprinted in my brain. To this day I associate the smell of heavy diesel with adventure.

Our goal was to continue a series of hydrographic casts off the Oregon coast. We would get samples of water and measure temperature from the surface to the bottom at specific depths. We'd stop and lower a long metal cable with a weight on the end. To it we attached Nansen or NIO (National Institute of Oceanography) sampling bottles at proscribed lengths of the cable by leaning over the side of the ship, grabbing the cable and aligning slots on the bottle with the cable. Then one hand would hold the bottle on the wire while the other tightened the retaining

5

screws. The text book photos I had seen were all shot in fair weather and calm seas and the job looked easy. But with 10-15' Pacific rollers coming at us, it was not.

Our second goal was to recover a lost current meter. It was attached to two or three railroad wheels as an anchor and a ground line that had been played out on the sea floor. The ground wire provided the recovery option we now needed. The float supporting the current meter either had broken free or sunk and now the expensive current meter was somewhere on the bottom. So between hydro casts we would drag a grappling hook across the sea floor hoping to catch the ground line. When it did, the tension on the grappling hook wire would jump and we would know we had hooked something.

The call came in the middle of the night. Most of the students were sea sick and no one wanted to climb out of a warm bunk and assemble on the deck in the driving rain and pitching seas. But up we went.

The grappling hook had found something and it was being reeled in on the Cayuse's boom. Shortly after I arrived on deck the hook rose out of the water to the snatch block at the end of the boom. Holding on with both hands I watched the hook pitch left and right as wave after wave lifted and dropped the 70' Cayuse. With each wave the two ends of the ground wire suspended above the deck by the hook rubbed against the stern of the ship adding a nasty rasping sound to the cacophony on deck.

Someone yelled to me that since we didn't know which end of the ground wire held the current meter,

6

we would have to cut the ground wire and haul in each end, one at a time. To do this we had to secure each end of the cable and then cut it between the two secured points. Then we had to clamp one of the two ends to another wire that would pull it in with a winch. In port this would be a tricky operation, out here it was madness.

The party chief, Asa, was a technician with years of experience. This was his time to step up and run the show. He did. He stood on the open stern of the Cayuse, balancing with no hand holds, with nothing between him and the open sea. He started to bolt a length of cable to one side of the ground wire. The ground wire slid and jumped and could have pulled him overboard at any second, but he pivoted and swayed as it moved and kept his balance.

Then it happened. It took a fraction of a second but burned a memory in my mind and in Asa's life jacket. Under the tension of several one-ton railroad wheel anchors, the grapple wire parted.

Freed from its load one end of the wire snapped upward, shattered the light atop the boom, then whistled through the block and tangled onto the winch. The cable had snapped back like a giant rubber band stretched beyond its limit. No one was hit.

But the other end of the wire held the grappling hook with its 5 ton load. It screamed downward heading for the sea bottom, but before it disappeared over the stern, it hit Asa and then slammed into the deck sending a shower of sparks into the sea.

I stood frozen. Frozen in disbelief and fear. Two seconds passed.

Asa turned toward the bow and yelled something I could not hear above the roar of the sea. A black burn mark on his orange life jacket was the only visible memento of this encounter with 5 tons of fury spearheaded by one of the prongs of the grapple. He was lucky. We were lucky.

That was my introduction to field science. I embraced the adventure then and still do, but try to remember Asa: I hang on tightly and look up. And, I ask myself if this is where I want to be standing.

Different research expedition: The RV Cayuse off the coast of Peru. To verify that the parachute drogue beneath the float had opened, I jumped into the water with my underwater camera. This was an El Nino expedition in 1977.

Towards the end of the one-year deferment Barbara and I married and moved to the East Coast for my Officer's Candidate School. Four months later I was an Ensign.

Under Fire

The Thompson sub-machine gun was invented by General John T. Thompson in 1918. It was as popular with World War II soldiers as it had been with gangsters in the era of prohibition. My first glimpse of one was in 1971 when we were conducting a repel boarders drill in the Western Pacific Ocean.

Fresh out of Officer Candidate's School my first duty assignment was as Executive Officer, Oceanographic Unit Three. The Unit sailed aboard a Victory ship, the MSNS Michelson, built in 1944. She had been mothballed twice before being pressed into service as the platform for collecting data to make maps for the ballistic missile firing submarines.

Barbara and I had just married six months before I boarded the Michelson in Yokosuka, Japan. We rented a house a few miles from the navy base in a small fishing village, Ashina. After a few days getting the most basic furniture and moving in, I left for my first 28-day cruise leaving Barbara to fend for herself not knowing anyone and not speaking the language.

One of my collateral duties was to hold emergency drills and one of them was repel boarders. We would gather our 22-man navy detachment on the fantail and practice shooting two Thompson sub-machine guns and some .45 caliber semi-automatic pistols. The crew loved shooting.

This wasn't an empty training exercise. The USS Pueblo had been boarded and taken three years before. Maybe we weren't as attractive a target as the Pueblo was, but we were shadowed periodically by Russian spy trawlers.

At the second repel boarders drill I loaded one of the sub-machine guns and aimed over the stern of the ship. I pulled back on the bolt handle and it locked in place. When I pulled the trigger all hell broke loose. A cartridge exploded in the chamber and sent part of the brass shell out the ejection port and across my face.

The gun was damaged. Blood was running down my face. Not knowing the extent of my injury I ran below decks to find the hospital corpsman. He wasn't in the clinic or his space. Someone yelled that he was playing rag ball on the number three hatch cover, so I climbed up to find him on the weather deck.

I emerged into the subtropical sunlight and squinted to see him. He was at the plate about to take pitch. I yelled, "Doc, I'm hit."

He looked over and yelled back: "Just a second sir, I'm up to bat."

Assured that my injury wasn't severe I waited until he hit the rag ball over the side of the ship ending the inning. I got a small scar on my cheek, but the Thompson wasn't so lucky. It was ruined.

Having completed my service obligation with the Navy I returned to graduate school in Corvallis, Oregon. Barbara enrolled in an MBA program and worked while I studied for my Master's and then PhD in oceanography. I went on several expeditions with Oregon State, the most significant one was spending part of a winter in Antarctica.

Living on Thin Ice

In late winter the sun was low in the sky and gave beautiful lighting to our stark surroundings. White - everywhere. Except for the "nunataks", black tops of mountains that stuck out above the snow and ice. Black and white, below the purest blue sky.

I would wander outside and take a deep breath of the air at 40 degrees below zero. It would burn the lungs, but feel so good, so pure. In less than two minutes I would be cold not wearing a parka, but until then I would just enjoy the scenery.

Our two huts are painted bright red so they stand out from a distance. No matter what direction you look no other building or structure is visible.

I am standing on frozen salt water that is six feet thick. The ice isn't smooth like a frozen pond or a skating rink. The surface is rough with blocks broken off here and piles of frozen snow there. Walking across this surface is ankle-spraining slow.

Looking towards land I see Mt. Erebus rising above all else. There is steam cloud above the mountain as it is an active volcano.

12

We are fortunate to have a vehicle. It's a small tracked vehicle, called a Track Master. It is fun to drive until your arms get tired. No steering wheel, it has an accelerator and two brake levers, one for each track. To turn left, you pull back on the left brake and let the right track push you around. We all wanted to be the designated driver at first, but now knowing how hard it is to drive we are less eager to volunteer.

Our tracked vehicle is plugged into our generator when its motor isn't on. Otherwise the oil in the engine would get too sluggish to circulate and anti-freeze in the cooling system would freeze. When this does happen we have to call McMurdo Station for help. Hours later a mechanic shows up with a jet engine heater to unfreeze the Track Master, our ride.

Outside our two wanigans (huts on skis) is our stash of food. It's frozen solid. There are no animals here to gnaw on it, so everything is safe. No flies, mammals, no nothing except for one emperor penguin that waddled through our camp one day. It gawked at us, posed for some photos, and then waddled off in the wrong direction. He headed for land instead of open water that was 60 miles away.

It's odd that there is no life, except humans, where I stand. But six feet below me is a rich environment with seals, fish, starfish, clams, and much more.

To cook, one of us takes an ax or pick outside and breaks off a few steaks. Brought inside and left atop the heater they thaw. Cooking is done on a two burner Coleman camp stove. Just like our canoe trips at home.

We also have cans of fruit and vegetables on shelves inside. Care must be taken not to spill the liquid on opening the cans. Once any liquid lands on the deck it freezes and turns the deck into a slip-and-slide.

We work and eat in one wanigan – the one with a hole in the floor through which we lower our instruments. This is where we spend most of our time. The other wanigan is our bunk house. Two sets of bunk beds. The top bunks are always hot and the bottom bunks are cold. The deck is freezing. What we need here is convection and after a few days we requisition a fan from the station.

We have a radio to communicate with McMurdo Station. At 5 PM we are scheduled to call the base every day. After the first few days we stop calling as they aren't answering our calls.

On the left is our electrical generator; number 7 is our eating and working wanigan; number 4 is our sleeping wanigan.

Once in a while neighbors will drop in. Or, someone from McMurdo Station will come by to check on us. These visits occasion a few drinks and then a few more drinks, and a lot of merriment. Then they leave and we watch them disappear into the whiteness.

At first the cold soaked through our parkas. The thought of it brought hesitation before we ventured out. But after a couple of weeks the cold seems less harsh. Working outside requires taking off parkas and hats. But once we stop working and the sweat evaporates, the parkas come back on.

How cold was it? Most of the time it was -20 to -40 degrees. One day it got down to -65 F. One day the wind chill was -135. On that day we stayed indoors.

Our wanigans with Mt. Erebus erupting in the background

Digging a Hole in the Ross Sea

In one episode of the 1950s television comedy "The Ernie Kovacs Show" Ernie Kovacs sat on a tree branch on the set. With saw in hand, he started to the cut the branch on the wrong side – the side nearest the tree – with him sitting on the outboard side. Everyone knew what was going to happen when he cut through the branch, but of course it didn't. Completing the cut, he reached out and pushed the tree trunk down. Away it fell, leaving him sitting on the branch floating in air.

The thought of the Ernie Kovacs skit kept racing through my mind. I was standing in a shallow, square hole in the sea ice of McMurdo Sound, Antarctica. My job was to dig to the bottom of the ice so we had access to the water below. Then we could lower our water collecting bottles, current meter, and conductivity probe to the bottom of the sound.

I'm standing on the only thing that is keeping me dry and I'm happily sawing away. I'm cutting square foot blocks of sea ice with an electric chain saw and prying them free with an ice chisel. What happens when I get to the bottom of the ice six feet away? Am I sawing the branch I'm sitting on and if I am, will Ernie Kovacs help?

We were rookies at cutting holes in ice. We were oceanographers used to having blue ocean beneath us, ready to accept whatever scientific apparatus we dropped in. In Antarctica however, there was a frozen road block we had to get through first.

We thought we might melt our way through the ice. The mechanics at McMurdo Station rigged up a 55 gallon drum with a hand pump. We would attach a hot air blower into the drum to send a stream of super-hot air onto the ice and pump out the melt water.

The hot air blower we borrowed from the base was a blower used to warm engines on airplanes so the hydraulic and fuel lines won't freeze. A worker from the base drove the heater out to our wanigan, our hut on skis. He fired it up and we placed the drum in a hole in the wanigan floor and prepared to pump.

Nothing happened.

The wanigan got hot. The thermometer inside topped out at 150 degrees, while outside it was nearly-50 below. So Rocky, our team electronics technician, and I stripped and engaged in the Antarctic tradition called the 200 Club. This entails running, naked while experiencing a 200 degree temperature change.

While we were running around on the sea ice the airplane heater was blowing hot air causing barely a dribble of ice to melt. Clearly we weren't going to melt our way through the ice.

We checked with the base logistics shed to see what they might recommend. They came up with a heavy duty auger. It had huge, aggressive teeth and was powered by a gasoline engine. We hauled it into our wanigan and into the future ice hole. Secured in place and with the engine running the auger spun around and around.

17

We let it spin while we cooked dinner. After we ate we noticed the auger had not moved one inch. We loaded lead weights on top in the hope that would speed up the digging. It didn't.

Back at the logistics shed we checked out an electric chain saw. This didn't sound like a good idea. What happens when the electric chain saw meets the salt water? How do you dig a hole through a layer of ice you're standing on?

Henry, our team leader, started off. He made vertical cuts in the ice and jammed the ice chisel into the cuts to crack out a cubic foot ice cube. Then he lifted the cube up and onto the wanigan floor so we could slide it out the front door.

It took more than an hour for Henry to cut out the first layer of ice blocks. I took over for the second layer.

Removing the first block of each new, deeper layer was tricky. Once it had been removed, the subsequent blocks could be pried into the now open space. Like a sliding tile puzzle. But getting the first one free was tough. I would pry here and cut there until pieces of the first block could be extracted.

By lunch time I was down three feet below the top of the ice surface. Noon sunlight lit up the ice hole with a beautiful blue tint, the light coming from the ice outside our wanigan. The sun quickly set while we ate lunch and I got back in the hole all afternoon.

Down five feet I was thinking more about how to escape from the hole when I did break through to the water below. I imagined it would come gushing in to fill the hole in seconds. Meanwhile I'm standing, not dressed for a swim, then treading water while holding an electric chair saw. With the power on.

Henry had thoughtfully rigged up an escape rope. He tied loops into a long rope and secured one end to the gantry pole above the ice hole. Would I be able to pull myself up hand over hand with wet clothing and boots filled with water?

Deeper I dug. Cautiously I kept sawing and prying and lifting ice blocks over my head to reach the wanigan deck. Then I noticed water seeping into the bottom of the hole. I threw the chain saw and ice chisel up and out of the hole and clambered as fast as I could to get out of the hole and onto the wanigan floor.

Safely on the wanigan deck, I peered down into the hole to check the water flow. Not a gusher. Not a flood. Merely a trickle of water flowed into the hole. The water was oozing through a porous layer of ice at the bottom of the hole. There was still a few inches of ice to be removed.

I lowered myself back into the hole with the chain saw and dug a couple more inches of ice. Finally as the water level was rising up over my boots, I climbed out again.

Standing on the deck of the wanigan we took turns breaking the last few bits of ice with the ice chisel. It was hard work lifting the steel bar and slamming it

19

down without losing grip and losing the chisel to the ocean below.

At the end of the day we had our hole and the science could begin.

I'm using the ice chisel to break out a block of ice

How to Go at 40 Below

One of the many challenges of spending winter months in Antarctica is meeting the necessities of bodily functions. McMurdo Station was well equipped with facilities to keep you warm while you go and to handle waste safely. But out in the wild it's a different story.

We set up our research camp on sea ice in McMurdo Sound a few miles from the US base. We had two wanigans, sheds on skis, to house our work and sleeping quarters.

The wanigans each had their own oil heater. Those heaters put out heat enough to cremate Sam McGee. One of our initial problems was regulating the temperatures inside the sleeping wanigan. Marilyn occupied one top bunk and I had the other. Five feet above the wanigan floor temperatures climbed to 90. Rocky and Henry had the bottom bunks a foot off the floor where temperatures were near freezing. The first few nights in the sleeping wanigan had Marilyn and me climbing down from the top bunks throughout the night to lower the thermostat on the heater. Rocky and Henry soon followed us, but raised the thermostat as they were cold. Up and down we climbed all night. After two or three nights we figured out the solution and requisitioned an electric fan from the logistics shed on base. It mixed the air so we all could be comfortable.

The most annoying problem was how to go at 40 below. Some modesty was required as we were a team of three guys and Marilyn. She was one of only two women on the continent and the only woman working in the field.

Admiral Dufek, the guy in charge of the US Antarctic research program during the 1950s, pointed out the difficulty of extracting a short member through many inches of clothing and parkas. Still we had it much easier than Marilyn.

Marilyn shovels snow that we will melt on the stove for drinking water. Don't eat yellow snow.

The three guys would pee onto the snow and ice surface surrounding the wanigans. After a few days the streaks of yellow snow made the job of collecting snow for drinking water more tedious as the collector had to venture farther and farther. We did learn to focus our efforts in one area to keep the rest of the area clear.

More problematic was how to poop. We had been issued a canvas tent, a collapsible toilet seat, and a small garbage can. Instructions were to use a plastic liner in the can and bring the filled liner back to base for disposal. The can with liner would be kept in the tent that provided both some privacy and a wind shield, but no heat.

We set up the tent between the two wanigans. For safety in a white-out, we strung a hand line supported on bamboo poles between the three structures. If visibility were to drop to zero, we could still walk safely between the wanigans and the canvas tent in a storm. People have died getting disoriented in a whiteout and wandering off into the blizzard.

To use the tent facilities, we would have to get onto hands and knees on the snow/ice surface. Gloves were removed so cold hands could untie the tent straps that secured the flaps. Then we would crawl headfirst through the narrow opening into the tent. In the cramped interior of the tent the toilet seat sat at nose level as we crawled in. Completing your entry required twisting around and then re-tying the flaps securely. Finally, with drawers dropped you would rest your naked butt on the plastic seat that was chilled to the ambient temperature, 40 below.

Thinking of the entire process was worse than doing it, but thinking was enough to demand creative improvement. First, Marilyn got on the radio and in her sexiest voice complained to the base crew that her bottom was cold from sitting on the plastic toilet seat. As you might imagine the entire base of 100 navy guys, who had not seen or talked to a women in months, were highly motivated to help. They stampeded to be the guy to solve Marilyn's problem. The winning entry was an orange faux fur cover for the toilet seat.

Things improved from there. We figured out we could keep the plastic toilet seat in one wanigan so it stayed warm while the can stayed outside with its solidly frozen contents.

Our butts avoided frostbite. Problem solved; now we could focus on the science.

The solution to our problem is in Henry's hands.
Marilyn, Rocky, Henry (seated), and me

This Isn't Going to End Well

The neighbors invited us over for dinner. A nice gesture. They were camped a few miles from us. Both camps were floating on six feet of frozen sea water. This was late winter in McMurdo Sound, Antarctica.

I wanted to think that they were anxious to have the company of all four of our crew. That would not be the case, however. It was Marilyn they wanted to have visit.

Marilyn was a vivacious, buxom, in-your-face, redhead and one of only two women on the entire continent. The other woman was a nun stationed at the McMurdo Navy base. Marilyn was popular.

The others in our crew were Henry, chief scientist, expedition leader, and physical oceanographer. Rocky was an instrument technician. I was a physical oceanography graduate student. Marilyn was a biological oceanography graduate student. That's us. We lived in two wanigans, tiny sheds on skids that could be dragged across the ice. One we slept in and in the other we cooked and did our research.

Weekly, we made trips across the sea ice into "town," the navy base at McMurdo. We'd take our weekly shower, watch a movie, buy something to drink, and pick up supplies. We stored food on the ground outside our cooking/working wanigan. With no animals to bother it and with temperatures 20 – 40 below zero food required no other protection.

On one of our town trips we met the two guys in the next camp. They were two atmospheric scientists from Colorado. They came over to our camp one night for dinner and too much wine, and they reciprocated by inviting us over the following week.

We cranked up the tracked vehicle and headed across the ice. Although we couldn't see their camp from ours, we knew generally where they were. After a few minutes of slow driving we spotted their wanigans.

These guys knew how to cook and put our meager presentation to shame. In our defense Henry did not cook – he was the leader of the pack and leaders don't cook. Marilyn didn't want to cook and appear to be our expedition's female assistant. Rocky wasn't wild about cooking either and that left me. Typically for dinner I'd retrieve some steaks or shrimp by knocking apart the frozen supplies with an ax. Our stove was a two-burner Coleman white gas stove, and everything I cooked was fried.

But our hosts that night had located some supplies on base that we didn't know existed, and they were extravagant in their selection of wine – both in quality and quantity. Dinner was great. Until.

It was about -40 outside and inside was a toasty +70. We had stripped off parkas, hats, and boots and were mid-way through dinner when the first explosion occurred.

The loud bang was followed by billowing black smoke that filled the wanigan. We opened the door and ran outside expecting the wanigan to burst into flames.

It didn't. So after a few minutes with the door open the air inside cleared out. No damage was visible so we clambered back in and resumed dinner.

Kaboom number two sent us flying out again. We waited in the -40 degree temperature for the air inside to clear. Then for a second time we ventured back in to finish our dinner.

The third explosion convinced us that something was definitely wrong and that we should forgo dinner. Someone tried to radio the navy base to suggest that they send out a fire truck. No one answered our call of distress, so we were on our own.

When the air cleared again one of the Colorado guys went inside and shut off the oil-burning heater. That ended the explosions. It also ended our dinner as inside the temperature quickly dropped to 40 below.

Not quite full, we grabbed our gear and headed across the ice for home.

It turns out that the tube feeding oil into the heater had developed a small hole. It dripped oil onto the metal pan beneath the heater. When the pool of oil was large enough and hot enough it exploded. Then it would take several minutes to leak enough oil to repeat the explosion.

No harm done. Marilyn grew closer to one of the Colorado guys, breaking at least 100 hearts at the navy base. We finished our work as the season changed to spring, and we left for home.

If you ever find yourself in Newport, Oregon, you might run across Marilyn's name. The library at the Oregon State University Marine Science Center is named for her: Marilyn Guin. My teammate; one of only two women on a continent the size of the US; and a very lively lady.

Marilyn runs a hydro cast by attaching the yellow
Bottle to the wire and lowering to collect a water sample

With my master's degree in hand I plunged into the PhD program at Oregon State. One day I noticed a hand-written letter thumb-tacked to the bulletin board of the Oceanography Department. The letter was from a navy captain who needed help sailing his new boat across the Pacific Ocean. This sounded like a cool adventure so that night I mentioned it to Barbara not expecting her reaction: "Yes, let's do it."

Sailing Across the Pacific Ocean

We arrived in Japan June 16, 1976 with a target sailing date of July 4. The two weeks on land re-acquainted us with Yokosuka, where we had lived five years before, and gave us time to learn the rigging and sailing characteristics of the *Enterprise*.

The *Enterprise* is a 54' long ketch that had just been built in Taiwan to the owner's specifications. A ketch is a sailboat with two masts. The forward mast is taller. The after mast is located forward of the rudder post. Yawls, which look similar, have the after or mizzen mast behind the rudder post. The advantage of sailing a ketch is that there are lots of options in matching wind conditions to the sail plan and no one sail has to be so large that it's difficult to handle.

We sailed in Yokosuka Bay, bought groceries at the navy base commissary, and had time to explore. That included a visit to our old house on the far side of the Miura Peninsula in a community called Ashina.

We purchased 203 raw eggs to take along and coated each one in Vaseline to keep it fresh. Food was stored in lockers in the main cabin and the tiny freezer in the galley was stuffed with frozen meat and a bit of ice cream dedicated to celebrating a birthday.

The crew included the captain/owner Arch; his wife Mary; and their fourteen year old son, Craig. The other crew was a retired navy chief, Ray. Arch was about to retire as a captain in the navy and we assumed that meant years of experience with ships and boats. Turns out Arch was a naval aviator.

Personalities were on collision courses and that became obvious even before we set sail. Arch dreamed of sailing around the world and telling his story to National Geographic and everyone else. In his story he was the hero.

His wife, Mary, really didn't want to be there. She got seasick easily and didn't like to sail. But she answered the wife's call of duty and agreed to go.

Craig wanted to play professional baseball. He was concerned that with all this sailing he might miss a season. Somehow he never had that discussion with his father.

Ray, the retired navy chief, was a competent sailor who knew what he was doing at sea. For 20 years he had been taking orders from officers who didn't know what they were talking about and quite frankly he wasn't going to do that in retirement. He spoke his mind freely regardless of consequences.

Barbara and I, of course, were perfect and had no hang ups to share. Honestly we provided calm voices and willing hands – most of the time.

On June 25 Barbara varnished a boom, the sail maker came aboard to sew hanks on our staysails, and Ruby became a typhoon. One week later she gained her maximum winds, 120 MPH while moving to the northeast, south of Japan. Then she moved up along the coast of Japan. We delayed sailing one day to avoid her wind and waves. We should have waited longer.

July 5, 1976. Up at 0230 and away from the dock at 0400 we sailed south through Tokyo Bay to the open sea. Unbeknownst to all, we had a diesel fuel leak in the main cabin. The fumes coupled with very rough seas laid up four of the six crew. Arch stood his watch for several hours and then he and I alternated one hour stints at the helm.

As we turned northward in the Pacific Ocean we had following seas of 30'. At least that is how I remember them. Swell would lift the stern and the Enterprise would slide down the steep face of a wave. A small mistake on the helm would turn us sideways in the trough of a wave which would spell disaster when the next crest arrived. Fighting to stay alert and keep the boat from turning sideways was a harrowing experience.

The seas did calm, the crew overcame their seasickness and life was more enjoyable. We even used the motor sometimes when there was no wind.

We got into a cycle of dead calm, rising winds, whistling winds, and back to dead calm all in the matter of one or two days. Each change in the wind dictated a change in the sails so we were busy furling and unfurling.

At the helm on a nice evening in the North Pacific

One day we enjoyed eerily calm wind and no seas or swell. The ocean surface was a mirror. We were becalmed. Ray and I grabbed the boat's tiny dingy, hopped in and rowed out 100m to take some photos of Enterprise. We didn't get very far before noticing that the dingy was leaking like a sieve. One of us rowed while the other bailed until we got back on board Enterprise.

Mary was sick often so Arch stood some watches alone. On a couple of occasions he would call her to prepare meals even when she was sick. Barbara and I offered many times, but Arch would drag Mary out of bed. We did wrestle meal preparation away on some occasions. Each Saturday night we made pizza. With the small size of the oven we made one three-person pizza at a time and ate in shifts.

Arch enjoyed smoking cigars and a pipe. Mary asked him not to smoke cigars in the cabin and he made that concession, but continued to smoke his pipe in the cabin. He was in his own world. Once or twice he left the official ship's log open and we could read how he described the trip. From our perspective there wasn't much correlation with reality.

As an example, late in the voyage our intended course was due east, 090. Barbara and I adjusted the sails to this course and then sailed the ship according to minor changes in the wind. Sometimes 075, sometimes 100, but we tried to keep the sails full rather than luffing to maintain due easting. Arch didn't understand this and would yell at us. In the log he claimed that:

33

…we sailed 32 NM to gain 5 NM along the established track. Instead of trimming and or changing sails to maintain ordered heading, the watch sections altered heading to suit the change in wind direction.

His wild claim would mean that we had sailed an average of over 80 degrees off course.

Arch annoyed everyone. Mary and Ray annoyed each other. Ray was happy to distribute criticism wherever he felt it should go. All in all, camaraderie had abandoned ship.

As we sailed north and westward the weather cooled. We had packed our long underwear and sweaters in addition to slickers. Arch and family weren't well prepared. The Enterprise had no heaters so the temperature inside the cabin was the temperature on the water, usually in the 50s. Only when we got to chilly Adak, Alaska did they get some warmer clothing at the navy Base Exchange.

Arch had assumed it would take two weeks to reach Adak, our refuel and resupply point. We would sail a great circle route and the Kuroshio Current would push us along. In reality the current has eddies that push forward today and oppose tomorrow, so it took us three weeks to get there.

Getting close to Adak we saw spectacular wildlife. Twice a lone seal greeted us hundreds of miles from any shore. The seals surfed in waves toward us, and they dove and swam back to catch another wave. Several times we sailed through large schools of dolphins. One night we were surrounded by many hundreds of spinner dolphins jumping out of the water. We were so stunned by their performance no one would go below to get a camera.

Sea otter appeared a few times near the Aleutians. As we were sailing up to Adak we sailed past a raft of maybe 200 sea otter.

We also passed some ships. A few were Asian fishing boats. Twice in the middle of the night we passed freighters. One required us to dodge out of the way. Although we had radar reflectors up on the mast, the quartermaster and bridge watch never saw us.

We lost track of the time zone we were in and thought we were arriving in Adak at midnight. Turns out it was 2 AM. To help us find the dock in a thick fog, a navy base fire truck was brought down to the dock and they turned on all their flashing lights for us to see.

We motored into a set of finger piers that were spaced about 40' apart. Arch was at the helm, but he lost control and almost got us wedged between two docks. Ray had been holding the bow line ready to make us secure to the dock. He dropped the line and yelled at me to get the line while he ran aft and pushed Arch away from the wheel. He recovered and brought the ship smartly into the dock. From that point onward whenever the sailing was difficult, Ray took the helm and Arch went below.

The three days in Adak were a relief. We enjoyed our first hot showers since leaving Japan, solid ground under our feet, a change in menu, and the chance to get away from one another – all good! Barbara and I met with some friends from my last navy base, Pacific Beach, Washington, and had a great time with them. We went fishing one day and watched orcas swimming by just beyond where we were throwing our lures.

On leaving Adak we motored through Kagalaska Strait, leaving the Bering Sea. I was at the helm. The tidal currents can be fierce in this pass, sometimes greater than 5 knots. At one point of our passage we hit a whirlpool: the boat spun around 360 degrees without me turning the wheel. We motored in, spun around, and motored out of the whirlpool. Back in the Pacific Ocean, we headed south.

Conditions on the boat quickly returned to the way they had on the last week of the previous leg. That is to say, not friendly. Barbara and I had the 8 – 12 watch morning and night and were somewhat isolated from the discord, if you can be isolated while always within 50' of others. We resolved to jump ship in Seattle rather than accompany Arch to San Diego, which had been the plan. Enough is enough.

Hundreds of miles off the west coast we were getting radio stations in Oregon and Washington. We had been away from home long enough to enjoy hearing news, sports, and weather.

Our voyage was years before GPS, so we relied on LORAN A and C, a radio direction finder, and dead reckoning. Ray and I tried celestial navigation twice, but it was difficult from the deck of our bouncing sailboat and we had good sunset star viewing only a few times.

We found our way into the San Juan Straits and were enjoying a rare sunny, warm day. Arch wanted to motor in the strait, which he did until the engine quit. We figured that we had drained the first fuel tank and had to switch to the second tank. Arch insisted that he would make the switch.

The engine still didn't start so he decided there must be an air block in the fuel line. He sucked on that fuel line for the better part of an hour. Dizzy with inhalations of fuel vapors, he gave up. Ray and I took his place in the small engine space. It took us awhile, but we discovered that Arch had not switched to the full fuel tank and had been sucking on an empty tank. We switched tanks and off we motored. I would have loved to read Arch's entry in the ship's log that night.

We sailed past Seattle on a beautiful day. Unfortunately Arch, who spent a fortune on building the Enterprise, didn't bother to get navigational charts. Ray and I were sharing the helm when we rounded Bainbridge Island and found ourselves staring at the Bainbridge – Bremerton ferry towering over us. The ferry was traveling at 15 knots and immediately sounded that sound that mariners dread: in extremis. She sounded five short and a long, long sixth blast of her horn.

In Extremis means that we are going to collide unless you do something. We did.

One of us turned the helm hard to port to get us out of the channel and out of her way. As she passed us her master was on the bridge wing with binoculars trying to read our name and homeport. This was his channel and he didn't want us in it.

One more surprise awaited us. We had to pass under a set of high voltage wires. Enterprise has a mast height of 70' above the water. At the center of the channel the catenary arch of the wires looked a lot lower than 70', but we didn't have a chart to check. Without the chart we couldn't tell how close to land we could go without hitting bottom. We maneuvered as far out of the center channel as we thought we could and then continued. Ray was at the helm and as we passed beneath the wires, he pulled his hands off the metal ship's wheel. If we had hit the wires it probably wouldn't have mattered if was touching on not, but it was the only safety precaution he could think of.

We had told Arch ten days before arriving in Bremerton that we were getting off there so he wasn't surprised. The day after we landed we off loaded our gear and put it into a rental car. Ray, Barbara, and I were about to hop in the car when Arch yelled out: "I get half of any royalties if you sell any stories about this trip. And, get to approve any articles before publication." This seemed like a funny time to bring up the subject and an awkward way to say goodbye, but that was Arch. We left.

PS. 43 years later Craig contacted us. Mary had recently died and he was going through some of her things and remembering our voyage together. He did get to play professional baseball, but not in the big league. Now he was a successful winery owner. Arch never got to sail around the world. Once they reached San Diego they sold the Enterprise. Ray? We don't know what became of him, but it sure would be fun to find out.

For several years in the 1980s Jim Henderson and I organized kayak expeditions to Southeast Alaska. The first year we ran the expedition through the Expedition Training Institute, now called the School for Field Science. They recruited ten college students to help us conduct research from kayaks. On subsequent trips we took smaller groups of adults. We recorded whale sounds from kayaks, measured tidal flows in the narrow inlets, and looked for transplanted sea otter. Mostly we loved being on one of nature's most beautiful settings with whales, otters, seals, sea lions, eagles, dolphins, and orca.

Years later I taught oceanography and environmental science for Semester at Sea. Barbara and I have sailed with them eight times: four full semesters and four shorter voyages.

Let a Sleeping Whale Sleep

People are intrigued by the question of "do whales sleep?" Or, "how do they sleep?" Whale sleep is not my expertise, but I've paddled kayaks next to sleeping whales twice. Once near Simon's Town, South Africa. I was teaching oceanography aboard the MV Explorer for Semester at Sea and took a small group of students on a kayak trip while the ship was in Cape Town. We saw lots of African penguins and a few seals; it was a nice paddle.

Paddling back into Simon's Town we heard deep sonorous sounds, but couldn't see where they were coming from. There was just enough chop on the water surface to hide the origin of the sounds. But then I noticed that I was paddling by the sleek black back of a southern right whale just two boat lengths away. On my other side was a second, smaller whale also fast asleep.

Our group paddled as quietly as possible passing the two whales so we didn't waken them. That was a wonderfully fortuitous experience.

Years earlier (1984) paddling ocean kayaks in Southeast Alaska we weren't as successful in letting a sleeping whale sleep. We were in Alaska to record gray whale sounds from kayaks and were possibly the first people to do this. It was commonly thought that grays didn't make sounds while feeding in Alaska.

One calm morning with the sea surface as flat as it could be, we were moving our camp to a new location. Paddling fast past some rocks, I was startled to have a sleeping whale wake up right beside me.

I didn't see the whale until it had moved. Two colleagues paddling behind me watched the whale raise its fluke, slap the water, and dive. It was a small gray whale spending its summer in Southeast Alaska.

We were as startled as the whale was. It was gone in a flash and we didn't see it again.

Do whales sleep? Absolutely. Can you wake them? If you're noisy or get too close you certainly can. It's best to let sleeping whales sleep.

Hit by a Whale

We had come to Sitka to record the vocalizations of gray whales. It had not been done before. I had surmised that trying to listen to whales talking or singing from a ship making noises from pumps, generators, and engines could be the wrong approach. We were going to listen from a quieter platform: ocean kayaks.

Three of us flew to Sitka and collected our kayaks. Jim Henderson had arranged for shipping the kayaks aboard a barge. We found our kayaks and got last minute supplies. To save time and energy we engaged a fisherman and his MV Fairweather to haul us and our gear 60 miles up the coast of West Chichagof Island to Baird Island.

We made camp on a small island and spent two days getting equipment checked out. The second afternoon a float plane dropped off Thane Tienson, the fourth member of our team.

Each day we paddled along the coast looking for whales. In previous years we had paddled the coast farther south and had seen only a few. But up here there were many. Most grays continue their northward migration into the Bering and even Chukchi Seas. Some aren't such ambitious travelers and prefer to summer in Southeast Alaska or British Columbia. This section of the coast has resident gray whales.

Unlike the other great whales, grays do not hunt for fish, krill, or shrimp. They alone scrape the sea floor,

42

sucking up mouthfuls of sand, silt, and hopefully some tasty worms and clams. They force the water and sand out of their mouths through their baleen plates and swallow what's left. So if they don't need sonar to find food, do they need to make sounds? Unlike noisy humpbacks that work in teams to corral food, grays feed alone and had not been recorded in Alaska.

Jim Schempp, one of our team members, had assembled a small hydrophone and recorder we could use from our kayaks. One person could listen to the sounds picked up by the hydrophone while they were being recorded. Another person could assist by stabilizing the boats from rocking in the swell. I was the lookout, trying to spot whales, get photographs, and predict where they were heading.

Jim Henderson looks for whales while Thane Tienson listens.

We paddled two days northward without seeing any whales. There were lots of otter, seals, sea lions, and bald eagle, but no whales.

From a base camp on Bertha Bay we set out and quickly found a whale in Davidson Bay. We heard him before seeing him as he came to the surface and blew. We set up to record him only to discover the recorder batteries were dead.

The next day, with fresh batteries, we ventured again into Davidson Bay. There, apparently, was the same whale. The recorder picked up sounds of him vocalizing along with miscellaneous sounds of sea lions and other animals.

We spent five days living in a tiny 11' by 11' cabin. Each morning as we wandered outside we'd find fresh bear prints around the cabin which convinced us we didn't want to sleep in tents here.

The last day in Davidson Bay we found our whale and were collecting recordings. Down he went for a feeding dive. I paddled to where I thought he would come up and waited. Jim and Thane were behind me making the recordings and Jim Schempp was fishing for our dinner.

I was holding onto my Nikonis underwater camera to catch a photo as the whale broke the surface. My paddle was resting on my spray skirt. Then the sea exploded into a thousand bubbles, like a giant bottle of champagne had been opened. I dropped my camera and grabbed my paddle as the kayak rocked.

The whale was surfacing directly beneath my boat. Sensing something in the water, it dove and re-surfaced a boat length ahead of me. You know whales are big, but seeing one this close made an impression on me. Luckily, I didn't roll over into the cold water and luckily my camera was tethered to the boat. No harm, no damage. But that was enough recording. We returned to camp.

Paddling back south to our rendezvous with the MV Fairweather we explored the White Sister Islands. A large colony of sea lions haul out there. The noise and smell travel far across the water. As we approached a few animals started to notice us. Then suddenly we had crossed some invisible line that sparked a defense. One giant bull barked and a dozen leaped into the water. As slow as they are on land they are furiously fast in the water. They came at us at flank speed and we paddled as fast as we could to get away. We had heard reports about sea lions attacking kayaks and didn't want any part of that.

Nearby, we also noticed a pod of humpback whales. They were feeding and breaching, but disappeared before we got close enough to record their sounds.

The following year we paddled out of Craig, Alaska. There we encountered many humpback whales, otters, and seals. That was a glorious expedition in outstanding weather, with none of the excitement of being hit by a whale.

Night of the Turtle

The odds were not in our favor: 70,000 of them and 15 of us. They had four-wheel drive and were highly motivated. But we weren't going to get pushed around.

At least we thought we wouldn't get pushed around. When a 90 pound sea turtle rams into your legs at flank speed it doesn't knock you down but does suggest you get out of the way.

They pushed, they shoved, and they crawled over top of their sisters to find that perfect piece of sand that would become their nest. If another turtle was in her path laying her eggs, so what. It was full "bring it on."

We were measuring shell (carapace) length, counting eggs dropped, and tagging flippers on Ostional Beach on the Pacific side of Costa Rica. Aside from a thousand stars shining in the clear night air, the beach was black dark. We wore headlamps, but until the nearby turtles were dropping eggs, the lights were off. The headlamps were wrapped in red cellophane to give us vision enough to record data without disturbing the nesting turtles.

The turtles, all females, were Olive Ridley sea turtles. Although their population is down to about 8% of its former size, it is the largest population for any species of sea turtles.

Once on the beach the female Olive Ridley turtles were focused on finding a spot to lay their eggs, digging a nest, laying the eggs, and getting back to the

46

sea. We 15 humans on the beach were haphazardly placed speed bumps slowing the performance of life's greatest task: Procreation.

I had brought a group of university students to help collect data on the turtles while they – turtles, not students - were laying eggs. The students were nearing the end of a circumnavigation studying with *Semester at Sea*. The turtles were returning to the beach where they had broken out of eggs their mothers had laid years before.

For some reason this 900 meter long beach is one of the most preferred beaches for Olive Ridley turtles. Several times in the late summer and fall, the females heave themselves up onto the beach to drop their eggs. All species of sea turtles do this, but not like the Olive Ridley does.

The magic of the night – the cause for the chaos of turtles crawling over each other and us – was an *arribada*. Arrival.

We had expected to observe and measure a few dozen turtles that night as the season for arribada was over. Or, so we thought. But this year there was to be a December arribada and our good fortune brought us here on the peak night.

Along this beach that extended less than a kilometer, 70,000 female turtles crowded ashore to find a patch of sand worthy enough to be their nest. If we had lined them up carapace to carapace along the length of the beach, they would have filled out more than 70 rows deep.

Nimble in water, sea turtles are clumsy on land. Each pull of the front flippers and push of the back flippers advances a turtle only a few inches up the beach slope. After an agonizing climb each must dig a hole about half a meter deep. The front flippers are spread and the rear flippers dig down, pick up a flipper full of sand and fling it. Some take 20 minutes to dig the hole deep enough.

Once a turtle starts to lay eggs, we could turn on our red-filtered head lamps. One student would dig a small trench directly behind the turtle so he or she could see the eggs drop out of the oviduct into the nest. If this was an invasion of privacy for the turtles, they didn't show it. With clicker in hand the student would count how many eggs were laid. Typical numbers were about 90 per nest.

While one student was recording the number of eggs laid, others were measuring the length of the carapace and flippers. We looked for the small metal tag on front flippers indicating that the turtle had been measured before. We also placed new tags on a few dozen turtles that night.

My biggest job that night was turtle wrangler. When a turtle was headed directly for one of our students counting eggs, I tried to redirect it. I'd pick up the front of the shell and point it in a different direction. Released from my wrangling, the turtle would move steadily in the new direction until it found its right patch of sand.

Once relieved of her eggs, a turtle refills the hole and stomps to compact the sand and hide the location of the nest. Competition to feast on the eggs can be fierce as vultures, coyotes, and humans eagerly dig up the nests.

The Ostional Beach is special because it is home to this arribada. It is also special because of a grand experiment being carried out. Locals have formed a cooperative to harvest the eggs. The morning after the arribada, dozens of locals came down to the beach shortly after sunrise to gather eggs. They took about 200,000 eggs in 50 pound sacks that morning. They drove the eggs to San Jose to sell to bars where they are eaten raw.

Out of the nearly seven million eggs laid that one night locals took 200,000. That's less than 3%. For the exclusive right to harvest the small percentage of eggs, the villagers provide security to prevent outsiders from taking them all.

Is it better to allow a small harvest to protect the majority of the eggs? That's the grand experiment. It

49

has been going on for several years and the population estimates so far suggest that it is working. We hope so.

After the turtle egg harvest in the morning, our group walked the beach. Someone discovered a newly-hatched baby turtle from the arribada of the previous month. It was having a tough time navigating through a pile of beach debris. One of the students, Quincy, picked it up and took it to the water's edge. Still not sure that the turtle would survive the surf zone, he held it aloft and swam out beyond the breakers before releasing it.

The arribada is one of nature's grand spectacles, albeit one that occurs in darkness making it hard to take in. Just being on the beach with 70,000 pushing and shoving and struggling turtles following the reproductive call of nature was moving. I know it had a profound effect on me, and I bet it is a lifelong memory for our students.

Andrew and I kayak among the bergs in Prince William Sound

Shark!

Don Koller and I were swimming back to his boat when the first shark hit. We had been pleasure diving all day and had seen only a few sharks at the very edge of visibility. This one had approached from behind us as we were finning along at dusk.

We were diving near West End, Grand Bahama with our families. Don and I decided we needed some fresh fish for dinner so we grabbed spear guns and jumped back in.

Currents had carried us about 200 meters from the boat in half an hour. In that time we caught a nice hogfish and several smaller fish. We had plenty for dinner, so we started back.

Half way to the boat the first shark hit. Don was towing a mesh bag that held the fish we had speared. The shark grabbed the bag and tried to swim away. Don felt the tug on the bag and without seeing what had caused it instinctively jerked the bag towards him.

We both turned around to see the shark swimming away at flank speed. We looked at each other as if to say, "What the hell!"

Doing a 360 degree search didn't reveal that shark or any others. The shark was gone. We continued towards the boat.

Just a minute later another, larger shark came up from behind us and grabbed the bag. Don again wrestled it from the shark's jaws and it swam away.

We looked at each other again. We were very close to the boat and would get there in just a couple of minutes. That seemed like the best option. But as we did another 360 search we changed our minds.

The first shark was back. So, too, was his larger brother. This time they didn't seem to mind that we saw them. They were swimming just a few meters behind us.

Decision time. How badly do we want fresh fish for dinner? How determined do we think the sharks are?

Don opened the bag and was turning it inside out when the larger shark flashed towards us, grabbed the bag and swam away. The smaller shark was in hot pursuit.

No fish dinner. No mesh bag. No shark bite.

Bigger shark, different ocean. Oceanic White tip, Red Sea (Photo by Fran Grenda)

Sweetwater Paddling

Busted by Customs Inspectors

Barbara and I had just returned from our trans-Pacific sail and were having pizza with some paddling friends, Tom and Shirley. After we recounted the highlights of our sailing adventure, they described a canoe trip they were planning. They were leaving in a few days; would we like to join them?

The trip was to paddle the Willamette River from Corvallis to Portland. The Willamette is a peaceful river that cuts through the heart of the Willamette Valley. It passes through several small towns and the state capital, Salem. This valley is why settlers came west in the 1840s.

Although we hadn't fully unpacked from our sailing adventure we agreed to join them.

We shuttled a car to Portland to bring us home and bought food for the three night trip. We camped in a state park one night and on tiny islands in the river the other nights. The trip was relaxing; the weather was gorgeous; and the company was delightful.

The last day found us struggling against strong head winds as we paddled through downtown Portland. To give some shelter from the wind, we got as close to the west bank as we could. At one point we paddled within a few feet of a small freighter from Brazil that was unloading cargo.

A mile down river we noticed two police cars with lights flashing above the west bank. Below the police cars was a small crowd of people staring at us. One of the men yelled, "Come over here. We want to talk to you."

Not at all sure we wanted to talk to them, we paddled closer but maintained a safe distance from the dock.

"US Customs," the man said. He flashed his badge. "We need to search your canoes."

What? We hadn't been outside the country.

Dutifully we pulled over and held onto the dock. One of the two agents started to step into our canoe. We yelled and he quickly got back on the dock. Clearly he had never been in a canoe before and would have tipped us over right there at the dock.

They told us that they had a call from someone claiming we picked up something that had been thrown off the Brazilian freighter. They thought we were part of a smuggling team and had contraband on board.

We showed the agents our waterproof bags and explained how difficult it was to open and seal them. They tried opening one and agreed that it would have been nearly impossible for us to open and close the bags while paddling against the wind.

Satisfied that we weren't smugglers, they were ready to leave. They told us this was the first time in the history of the Portland US Customs office that they

54

had inspected a canoe. I asked what they would have done if we had not complied with their request to pull over to the dock. One agent shrugged and said there was nothing they could have done. They didn't have a boat.

PS. Four years later I was telling this story around a campfire in Southeast Alaska. We had a team of ten college students with us doing surveys of sea otter from ocean kayaks. That day, one of our students had flipped over in a williwaw. The sudden wind gusts had knocked over her boat and landed her in the chilly water. A fishing boat nearby saw us struggling to rescue her and came over to help. They joined us for dinner that night and brought some salmon they had caught. As I told the story of being inspected by US Customs in Portland one of the fishermen jumped up. "I was there," he said. "I was on the dock that day." He lived in Portland and was attracted to the dock by the police lights and witnessed the escapade. Small world.

On another trip:
Completing the loop of Bowron Lakes, British Columbia

Yellowstone River Upside Down

Jim Chester, a fellow member of The Explorers Club, and I arranged three river trips to commemorate the bicentennial of the Lewis and Clarke Expedition. The first was on the Upper Missouri starting at Great Falls, Montana. The second was the Lower Columbia from Portland to Astoria and the last was on the Yellowstone River.

The low roar of water rushing past rocks alerts you to the pending maelstrom. Soon you see the white water piling up into pillows covering boulders and wave trains of standing water threatening not only your progress down the river, but your very existence.

You might decide to get out of the boat and scout the whitewater. With better, but not absolute knowledge you might decide to line your boat through the rapids or portage around. Possibly emboldened by what you see and with self-confidence spilling over the top of your kayak deck, you might decide to run the rapids. Then you could slide to the right or left of the biggest waves and squeeze through, either delighted to have survived or disappointed that you missed the excitement of meeting the wave head on.

Or, you could decide to take the rapids head-on. As you approach you may question your decision, but your course of travel can be difficult or impossible to change. Five knots of water flow over a shallow, paddle-biting bottom, makes last minute changes of heart meaningless.

Soon you are sweeping to keep the waves from pushing your bow off course. A wave lifts the bow and pushes it to one side. You pull hard to bring it back, to point downstream.

Then the center of the boat rises and the bow falls down into the trough. You're in the wave, not an innocent bystander, but part of the turbulent excitement. You and the river are one – even if you'd prefer an immediate divorce.

Your yells are drowned out by the roar of water. Contorted by waves crashing from the left, rising from the right, head-on and behind you, the boat creaks and groans, and the fiberglass crackles.

This was our fifth day on the Yellowstone River. Rapids and tranquil sections had passed and each new river bend brought new vistas of mountains, bald eagles, and irrigation pumps. I was taking photos of all three. Would you like to see my Yellowstone River irrigation pump photos?

Ron, the safety officer of our flotilla, had admonished us this morning with the word of the day: "complacent." He preceded the word with: "Don't be…." I focused on the word "complacent" and became what I thought about.

As sweep, my job was to ensure that everyone else got down the river ahead of me. If someone bailed, I'd be there to pick them up. If they lagged, I'd urge them onward. My job was to always stay upstream of the last paddlers. Usually, I did this.

But, sometimes I pulled ahead to catch a glimpse of the next section. Racing ahead of the others, I'd have to turn around and paddle upstream to wait for them to get through.

With a mostly waterproof camera I was taking photos while boating through rapids. As we approached, I'd assess the rapids to see if I could afford to take hands off paddle to snap pictures. Just upstream of the city of Columbus, the next rapid looked like a good one for taking photos. There weren't many more photo opportunities as Columbus was our take-out.

"Better snap some pics through this rapid," I thought.

Everyone else had successfully gone through the rapids or, skirted around the side. The skirting was the preferred option for most. Although the waves were 2-3 feet and we were in ocean kayaks not meant for white water, the boats were doing surprisingly well, punching through waves and remaining upright.

I pulled the camera out of my PFD (life vest) pocket and laid it on my spray cover. Then I paddled towards the left side of the rapids so I could shoot across the river, towards the right to catch the waves.

I laid the paddle on the deck and picked up the camera.

"Not yet. Wait for a better shot," I told myself.

Bow falling then rising, we (the boat and I) entered the first wave. From the trough of a wave I looked up

58

at the crest of the next wave. Land had vanished. All to be seen was water below and sky above.

Fellow paddlers must have been close by but I couldn't see or hear them. Now: click. Left hand holding the paddle, the right held the camera.

Looking back to the left, the water parted revealing a rock. A second before, it had appeared to be a standing wave sans rock. Now the lie was discovered a boat length away.

I dropped the camera onto the spray cover. With both hands back on the paddle, I pushed hard on one side and pulled on the other. But the aquatic gods of fate slammed my boat onto the rock.

At that terrible moment – balanced by water and rock - the dynamics changed.

Pushed where I could not go by a ton of water roaring at the speed of disaster, the rock stopped downstream progress.

My sense of balance shrieked panic.

The paddle flayed desperately, grabbing nothing but froth.

The starboard rose, the port held low. The stern swung instantly downstream while bow spun upstream and skyward.

A frantic draw on the right bought a moment. Nothing more.

59

In the time it takes sound to travel from throat to lips, the "aw shit" was lost in the chaos of water, air, boat, paddle and a world suddenly upside down.

Now it's darker and less noisy. Just as breathing was natural seconds before, now it is not. Lips lock shut without the mind being aware.

"Hat is still on (how did it stay on?)."

"Paddle is in-hand."

"Will we roll up? Not enough water for a roll."

"Strange: this is comfortable. Upside down is okay. No need to rush."

A rock zips by at 5 miles per hour and brushes the PFD.

"Where's the camera?" The right hand follows the strap.

Resting on the spray cover moments before, the camera now dangles down, almost hitting the fast moving bottom.

"Where's up?" Something rushes by – hard to see what.

No need to hurry. Nothing hurts. Grab the camera. I'll be pissed if I lose it. Moments before it was in the relative safety of my PDF pocket. Now it is bounding along, inches above the bottom held by a lanyard around my neck. I pull it up and grab it with my right hand.

We're going backwards.

The downstream side rises. And, then falls.

"No hurry, air holding, lungs feel good."

Without thought, the right hand reaches forward for the spray cover loop.

"No decision yet."

"Found the loop."

"Pull backwards to bail out – no, dummy, pull forwards and up – away".

"Long enough, we're not rolling. We're bailing out." Maybe the decision was never made, but maybe it was made long before.

From the relative quiet underwater I emerge into the total chaos of the surface: waves breaking over the boat and the river's roar.

I'm upstream, clutching the kayak combing with my left hand, which also holds the paddle. "This won't work."

The camera occupies my right hand. Pulled out to take photos through the rapids, I start taking pictures again.

What I see is not what I get. The camera reacts like a dog on a hot afternoon. It snaps the photo so long after I push the button that it's hard to tell what I'm getting. In the time it takes the electronics to capture an image, the image has changed a hundred times. Funny how the high speed digital world is way too slow for this placid life in the river.

A wave splashes into my mouth. "Panic? No, this isn't bad."

Vortices tug me downward. My lips have a freeboard of mere centimeters and each wave and wavelet spills into my mouth.

My PFD rides up as if it's trying to save its own life by escaping me.

On the left bank, behind an eddy there are two paddlers. They are standing there, yelling, hands cupped over lips, but I hear nothing from them. They stand still while I'm bouncing, weaving, swirling, sometimes above and sometimes below the surface.

"Kick hard. "

Whack! My knee kissed a rock – hard.

I instruct myself: "Pull the knees up. Push the feet downstream. Take a photo."

"What's that?" Downstream. It's my kayak seat! My seat has come out and is floating two yards below me. I should go get it. I'm screwed without that seat. I don't want to paddle the rest of the day without my seat.

How am I going to duck under the boat with the paddle and camera in hand, swim downstream and retrieve the seat? I'm out of hands. Better stay where I am, holding the boat. Staying upstream.

"Which bank to head for? Everyone is on the left bank. The river doesn't seem to care. Go left."

"Kick. Take a photo."

Below me is John. He's shouting – something.

He shouts again: "Is that your seat?"

"Of course, it's my seat. It's the seat you sat in two days before and broke. And, yes I appreciate that you gave it a temporary fix– using an empty tuna fish can from dinner and duct tape. That is my seat, tuna fish can and duct tape, please rescue it."

Not waiting to hear an answer from me, he goes for it: "I'll get your seat."

"Yes, please. Get the seat."

"I'll swim to the left bank, twenty yards away." But 20 yards in fast swirling waters with a half-ton of water in my boat to pull is really hundreds of yards away.

Kick and kick. Not much progress. I hear stuff inside my kayak moving around. On dozens and dozens of kayak trips, I've never tested those waterproof bags and containers. Now we'll see if they keep stuff dry.

"I hope nothing else has come out of the boat. "

John's back, with my seat resting on his deck.

"Okay," I yell, "Give us a push."

His boat hits mine from downstream. I kick. We're going downstream fast, but not towards the shore.

Barbara is upstream, behind me. She wants to take my paddle. "The paddle is okay, but maybe I'd better give it to her and free up one hand. I pull the paddle upstream and duck underwater to let it pass over my head. Now I'm holding the camera and paddle in my right hand and boat in my left.

I try to pass the paddle to her. We miss, still zipping down the river at Yellowstone speed. She back paddles to make another pass. I reposition the paddle too, but have to let go of the boat to do it.

John shouts," Can you take a tow rope."

"Yes."

On Barbara's second pass, we transfer the paddle. But I have to give up my hold on the boat and it has slid past. I grab the bow loop just before it drifts away. A second longer and the boat would have been out of grasp.

John tosses his stern line and I grab it, too. He pulls hard for shore but we make little progress.

I've drifted through the rapids and, if I don't get out now, I'll drift through the even more furious rapids below.

"Bad," I think. "Let's not do that."

Feet find boulders on the bottom and push while John is pulling.

Pull and push.

"Shallow water. Stand up." Fall down, push and pull.

"Stand up." At last my feet grab the bottom solidly and are able to hold on against the current. I pull the boat slowly towards the bank.

Bilge pump and bailer jump to work. Nothing else is missing. Boat emptied, seat returned, we scout the next rapid. It looks pretty cool.

Jim Chester and I check our location on the Yellowstone River

Now On Exhibit

For some reason the search committee picked me to be the director of the South Florida Science Museum. Their decision changed my life and the lives of our family.

Their selection launched my two-decade career directing museums. Running a museum was a learning experience unlike any other. I started out knowing nothing about museums and ended up lecturing on the subject of museum management and serving as President of the Ohio Museum Association. It was also an exhilarating experience. The Board of Trustees gave me the freedom to do whatever I wanted, as long as the museum did well. Once I figured out that I had that freedom and once I figured out what I wanted to do, it was a blast.

Busted in Peru

I was about to board the airplane in Lima that would take me home when he tapped me on the shoulder. As soon as I turned around, two men grabbed me and started dragging me away.

One hand held my travel bag and the other held the clothing bag for Mary, our Director of Marketing. She and Walter were in front of me about to board the plane.

The two men were yelling in Spanish and were quickly joined by a third man. He pushed from behind as the first two held my arms. When we arrived at a women's bathroom, one opened the door, shouted to

clear it out, and then pushed me in. I turned to see
the third man lock the door from the inside.
They were screaming at me, but I had no idea what
they were saying or what they wanted. One grabbed
my travel bag, opened it, and pulled out everything
that was inside. He flung the contents onto the floor.
Obviously, they were looking for something, and
luckily for me, were not finding it.

One started unbuttoning my shirt. I pulled away and
finished the job. The man behind me kept jabbing me
in the back to hurry up, while all three kept yelling
excitedly.

Earlier, I had seen two of the men in the concourse.
They appeared to be staring at me but I convinced
myself that they weren't. Now they were madly rifling
through my clothes, and as seconds ticked by they
grew only more agitated.

I was down to my underwear and trying to decide
where I would stop complying. If it came to fists,
three to one I would go down in a heap.

Another few seconds passed, and the tempo slowed
to a crawl. Their shouting stopped. They talked
quietly to one another. Finally, one motioned for me
to get dressed. I jammed my stuff back in the bag and
walked quickly to the airline gate. Walter and Mary
had made enough of a commotion on the plane that
the door was still open and I was able to board.

We were in Peru to arrange a huge exhibit of Incan
and pre-Incan artifacts for our South Florida Science
Museum. I had gotten permission to explore the

necropolis, Batan Grande in Northern Peru, to get background images and information on the origin of the pieces in the exhibit. This off-limits area is often robbed and its priceless artifacts are sold, many of which leave the country. This, I figured out later, must have been the reason for their search. They were customs inspectors hoping to catch foreigners walking off with gold masks, tumis, or jewelry.

The exhibit was a smash hit, generating long lines and overwhelmingly positive publicity. The final irony is what happened when the treasure did arrive at the Miami International Airport.

We were required to do a customs inspection. I met the plane on the tarmac. Seven police cars had encircled the airplane to guard the offloading of the $65 million worth of artifacts.

I walked across the tarmac to the plane. The 747's cargo door was open and a US Customs Inspector was standing there. We had asked our congressman to help intercede with US Customs and now it was time to see what he was able to do.

The exhibit was transported in 17 wood crates and I was afraid we would have to open each one to show the inspector the contents. I introduced myself to the inspector and asked him which crate he wanted to examine first.

He looked at the fleet of cop cars surrounding the airplane and growled: "Sonny, you get that goddamn shit out of my airport. I don't care what's in those crates. You just get it the hell out of here."

And, we did.

We ran off with $65 million of treasure without signing any documents and having any inspection. Much better than our custom's inspection in Lima.

Armored Car

To get the Incan treasure to West Palm Beach I called several armored car companies. At one company the public relations vice president was very much in favor of helping us. He offered to provide the car and guards at no cost in exchange for the publicity. All the museum had to do was pay for insurance.

That sounded great. I asked him to get a quote for the insurance. Two days later he called back: $25,000. That was about what we were paying to rent the exhibit. We couldn't afford that.

Instead we rented a small panel van for $40. One of the museum staff drove it onto the tarmac at Miami International Airport and next to the 747. Once the customs inspector told us to get out of his airport, we crammed the van with the wood crates.

With two Miami police cars in front and one behind, we drove north on I-95. At each jurisdiction border an exchange was made from police to sheriff or State Patrol. We and the police envisioned highway pirates lurking behind every parked car on the city streets. After a harrowing ride we got to the museum and off-loaded the treasure while six or seven very beefy and stern looking young police officers provided protection.

Not until the treasure was safely inside and I was ready to lock up the museum did I realize the mistake I had made. When looking to hire a security guard company to provide 24 hour protection, I had hired the cheapest company I could find. As the police officers waved good night I saw the 70 year old hired guard hobbling along to find a chair.

"What have I done?"

South Florida Science Center and Aquarium – formerly named the Science Florida Science Museum

Fire Alarms were Sounding

The phone call came minutes before 6 AM. A few minutes later I was in my car racing to the museum. The drive was short, but I was surprised not to hear fire engine sirens sounding already. I arrived at the museum before the fire fighters did.

No smoke was pouring out of the museum. No flames were visible. I felt the back door and it was cool to the touch, so I opened the door and turned off the horrible alarm. The smell of burning rubber filled the air. It wasn't until I was half way to the exhibit halls that I saw smoke.

This was the final day of a major traveling exhibit of Incan treasures. The exhibit had gone wonderfully well and had set new records for attendance, media coverage, and new memberships. Our financial gamble had paid off. Tomorrow, the exhibit would come down, and a few days later the worry of displaying $65 million of treasure would be gone.

The South Florida Science Museum did not employ guards, but for this exhibit we hired a security company to provide 24-hour on-site guards. Of course, I engaged the cheapest guard service I could find. This seemed like good management until the phalanx of state troopers, county sheriff's deputies, and West Palm Beach police officers left us alone with the treasure after escorting us from the Miami airport. Then I compared the professional demeanor and physical presence of these officers to the lone, aging guard that I had hired. My confidence withered.

But throughout the month-long exhibition we had only a few minor problems with security. During the first week the museum receptionist called me to say that one visitor was acting suspiciously. I walked out of my office to the exhibit hall and watched the visitor snapping photos of our security alarms.

I confronted the man and he quickly apologized. He gave me his business card: Supreme Court Judge for the State of Pennsylvania. He was a board member of a museum and was making notes on security in other museums while vacationing in Florida. So much for us being able to pick out the bad guys.

My first thought when I got to the museum that last morning was trying to get the artifacts to safety. But when I got to the exhibit hall, aside from the smell of burning rubber and some smoke, there was no fire visible. Then I remembered the security guard. The call I had gotten was from the alarm company, not the guard company. "The guard must have been overcome by smoke," I thought. So my focus changed to finding him.

I raced up to the second floor where the guard station was. Unlocking the door I found the guard...sound asleep. 10-15 minutes of blaring alarms and rancid smell had not awakened him.

The fire trucks arrived soon after. A belt had slipped off a pulley in the air handling room and had rubbed, creating the smoke and smell. There was no fire and we were able to open the museum that last day of the exhibition.

Next time I had to choose a guard service I didn't hire the cheapest one. But that didn't help.

On our Belize Coral Reef Health Expedition, holding the Explorers Club flag.

It Takes a Village to Catch a Thief

Florida State Museum officials watched over our shoulders as we inventoried the several dozen gold doubloons and pieces of eight they had loaned us for an exhibition of treasure recovered from Spanish shipwrecks. Our curator completed her tally and was two coins short. She patiently recounted the coins while the officials anxiously waited to take the coins back to Tallahassee.

She counted a second time and we were again two coins short. As she started, I began to wonder how we could have lost two coins.

The coins had been in our locked display case throughout the exhibition. Only the curator and I had keys to the case and there was no evidence of forced entry into any of the cases. She concluded her third count and was still two coins short. So we started the process of checking the serial numbers on the coins against the manifest. It took about 15 minutes to identify the two missing gold doubloons. They were valued at about $50,000 total.

The state officials were none too happy. We agreed that we had lost the two coins and would immediately search the museum for them. In truth, there weren't many places to search. The coins had been in my office briefly before going into the locked display case. Throughout the exhibition we had an armed guard from a private security company always within sight of the exhibit.

We filed a police report and as the news spread, rumors circulated: it had to be an inside job. This was a small museum, so fingers wanting to point at a culprit had only a few to choose from.

The exhibit had been exceptionally well attended and well covered by the media, so the writers and editors were primed to jump all over the story of missing coins. Each interviewer asked the obvious question: "How could you lose the coins? Who could have taken the coins?" I didn't have answers.

The evening after the story broke on television my next door neighbor, Neal, leaned over the fence to chat. He had heard the story and wanted to know all about the theft of the coins. I didn't want to talk about it, but did relent and gave him the same and only story I had.

The next day Neal called me at the museum. His sister's boyfriend worked in a pawn shop. A guy had walked in that morning wanting to sell two gold coins. Neal and the boyfriend had talked about the coins after my conversation with Neal.

"Hey," the boyfriend said to the man wanting to sell the coins, "aren't those just like the coins stolen from the science museum?"

That inquiry had sent the seller scurrying out the door. In an unsuccessful attempt to conceal the car license plate number, he drove backwards out of the parking lot. This was suspicious enough to call police. Luckily, the boyfriend had managed to read the license plate number of the fast disappearing car.

76

The police called me and asked if I recognized the name of the owner of the car. The name was not familiar at all. Two detectives went to his address and found him. Yes, he admitted, he had gone to the pawn shop. "Some guy" in Miami had given him the coins and asked him to sell them. He didn't know the name or address of the guy in Miami, but had managed to return the coins to him immediately after he left the pawnshop. So he claimed not to have the coins and not to know where they were.

The police asked a few more questions. Where, they asked, do you work? He replied that he was a security guard. Turns out he worked for the company that provided guards for our exhibit.

As the police told me about their interview with the presumed thief and former security guard, I remembered opening the display case one day so a newspaper photographer could get some shots of the coins without shooting through the display glass. As he was taking photos, I was called away to the front desk. So I had the guard stand by the open display case while I was gone. On my return I locked the case. In the few seconds I was gone, the guard took the coins.

The police didn't have enough evidence to arrest the security guard. But, a few days later a small package came to the museum addressed to me. Inside were the two gold coins.

What could have been a career-ending incident ended up being an anxious lesson in security measures. I'm glad I lived next door to Neal.

77

Free Snake with Your Call to 911

One strange afternoon at the South Florida Science Museum got much stranger. A boy came into the museum and asked if we had an outdoor wax museum in the park. "No," our receptionist told him, "why do you ask?"

He explained that there was a wax man hanging from a tree. I went to investigate and sure enough, there he was. Not wax, but he was hanging by a rope tied around his neck. His attaché case lay open near the base of a tree. He had been dead for some time.

I called the West Palm Beach police and they sent an officer. We talked and I ended up giving him a quick tour of the museum after he had filled out the paper work and made his calls. He left and little did I suspect that he would soon reappear.

Just before closing time the police dispatcher called the museum. They had a problem and wanted our help. The nice officer who had come by earlier had suggested the dispatcher contact us.

A 6-foot long Eastern Diamondback rattlesnake was discovered in the Intracoastal Waterway swimming along the seawall. The police would have to kill it if no one rescued the snake. The people at the zoo didn't answer their phone this late on a Friday afternoon, so the police called us.

With lights flashing and sirens singing my new friend the police officer sped me across town in his squad car. So far, this was fun. Awaiting us at the seawall was a crowd of a couple hundred spectators and a fleet of police cars with flashing lights. Still fun.

Two detectives had service pistols drawn and pointed at the snake as it swam along the sea wall. I lay down on the ground to get a look – it was the first time I had seen a rattlesnake outside of a cage. The two detectives stood on either side of me ready to blast it to snake heaven and scare the snot out of me. Not as much fun.

The snake was swimming in the water about three feet below the top of the seawall. I couldn't reach it and didn't really want to reach my hand down to grab it anyway. Pondering what to do, a local resident yelled out that he had a potato rake. That would help.

I grabbed the rake and leaned over the seawall to try to slide the rake under the snake. Over and over, I misjudged how quickly the snake could move. After each miss I jumped up and ran along the seawall to get ahead of it. Each time I moved, my cohort of over eager shooters moved with me. Not so much fun: I'm not liking the snake and even less the two guys bucking for lieutenant with their guns drawn.

Eventually I got far ahead enough of the snake to be in position as it swam beneath me. I picked it up with the potato rake and swung it over my head and onto the grass behind me. It was stunned and sat still long enough for me to pin it down to the ground with the rake.

The crowd went wild with cheers. This was a great show. This was fun.

79

But when their applause died away I was still stuck with a problem. I had a snake pinned underneath the rake and two armed and dangerous detectives trying to be helpful.

My only option was to grab the snake behind the head and stuff it into a canvas bag that had appeared. It took a minute to raise the nerve, but I held the snake in place with the rake and grabbed it with the other hand. In the bag and done.

The crowd cheered again. I'm much happier.

We contacted a (real) snake wrangler who showed up the following day. In a closed classroom at the museum I opened the bag so the wrangler could see the snake and get it into a proper carrying bag. As soon as the snake saw light, it leapt out of the bag and zipped around the classroom in a flash. It had rested overnight, was fully energized and wanted its freedom. We jumped atop tables to get out of its way.

The snake settled down after a minute, and the wrangler deftly captured it and hauled it away. Much, much happier.

Racing Tricycles Underwater

We organized an offsite event called *Seafest* for the South Florida Science Museum (SFSM). The idea was to draw people who were not museum goers to educational displays, presentations, and activities on the ocean and reefs of Palm Beach County. The challenge was to draw crowds large enough to make our efforts worthwhile and to keep the support of the commercial sponsor. Three wheels on the bottom of a swimming pool did it.

The PGA Sheraton Resort in Palm Beach Gardens offered to host the event. They would provide space, a few rooms, and some paid advertising. We, the SFSM, would organize the programming and keep any admissions we collected.

One of the tenets of Guerilla Marketing is to use your brains instead of your wallet to promote programs for nonprofit organizations. So we thought long and hard about how to hook media and generate public attention.

Underwater Tricycle Racing was born.

The resort bought several tricycles for us to conduct experiments. We immediately found it nearly impossible to operate the trikes underwater with our feet. Instead, we had to lean over the handlebars and turn the front wheel peddle by hand. Even then, the front wheel rose off the pool bottom and spun wildly, which stopped forward progress. We added 10 pound barbell weights to the handlebars to help keep the front wheel down.

We had thought that people could hold their breath while cycling underwater, but that didn't work. It took too long to cycle the length of the pool. So we used SCUBA equipment and limited contestants to certified divers.

Seafest opened and in the early afternoon we started the first heat. Pre-arranged contestants took turns racing head to head and scuffing up the bottom of the huge resort outdoor pool. Event attendees lined the sides of the pool and gawked at the frantic action of divers hunched over the handlebars desperately trying to keep the front wheel down on the pool bottom and spinning.

The winner of the women's races was my wife, Barbara. Her photo was shown across the US, around the world, and in National Geographic World magazine.

A week later, we got calls from a Japanese sports channel wanting to know when we would run the event again as they wanted to cover it.

Thousands of people attended *Seafest* and it generated thousands of dollars for the South Florida Science Museum. But it was a lot of work and drew visitors away from the museum that weekend. So that was the first and only time we ran *Seafest* and underwater tricycle races. Barbara has retired as an undefeated world champion.

Barbara winning the Women's World Championship in Underwater Tricycling.

Photo by Red Morgan

"Kick me" in Cairo

British Airlines had given the South Florida Science Museum several round trip tickets anywhere the airline flew as part of an auction we held. One ticket wasn't auctioned off so I used it to arrange exhibits for the museum. I traveled first to Egypt to set up an exhibit on toys and tools found in pyramids. Then I flew down to Kenya to meet Richard Leakey, then Director of the National Museum of Kenya, to negotiate borrowing casts of his early hominids.

It seemed like I had a sign on my back saying "Kick me." My first morning in Cairo I took a walk through the city. It was not long before a young man latched onto me and followed me around. His English was good. He said he wanted to practice it. Would I mind talking to him? I agreed.

He was friendly and talkative, and delighted to be speaking to an American. As we walked along, he invited me a dozen times to visit his brother's shop where I would find some amazing bargains. Eventually my resistance ebbed and curiosity rose enough to find out what his business was, so I agreed to follow him. "It's just around the next corner," he said. He said this about five times. I was about to give up when he announced we were there.

We walked into a building and went up to the second floor. When he had opened the door, my senses told me something was wrong. The air was thick with smoke, and it did not smell like tobacco. It took me a minute to realize that they were smoking hashish.

The young man who led me there introduced me to his older brother. The brother was sitting on a sofa with his arm draped around a young woman with blond hair. She did not seem to notice that I was there, or for that matter, that anyone was there. He rose to shake my hand, and mumbled something like "nice to meet you," before flopping back down on the sofa. Immediately he jumped up again, and repeated the handshake and greeting before collapsing a second time on the sofa. This seemed a bit odd.

I was becoming more and more uneasy. There were several other people in the room, but I could not tell what they were doing. I was beginning to surmise that everyone was stoned. Governments in the Middle East are tough on drug users and sellers. Visions danced through my head of the Cairo Vice Squad bursting through the doors, and dragging me off while I tried to explain, in English, what I was doing there.

Someone started showing me some jewelry he wanted to sell. Was this a legitimate jewelry business run by pot-heads, or something more sinister? Having heard and seen enough to satisfy my curiosity I remembered an important appointment and bolted for the door.

I found it odd that in both Cairo and Nairobi people approached me on the street only my first day there. In Nairobi, a young man approached me hours after I had landed. Like the young man in Cairo, he told me he wanted to practice his English: would I talk to him. This line sounded familiar. I figured I had an obligation to my cultural education to find out what his scam was, so I agreed. "Let's go to a cafe down the street," he suggested. At the cafe it became apparent that his first priority was to get me to buy him a meal. He kept suggesting that I order food. I could envision food arriving for the two of us, and me being stuck with the bill. I declined to order anything, but suggested that he might want to order. This annoyed him, but he proceeded to tell me his long tale of woe: he had fled the corrupt government of Uganda, and now was destitute and needed $80 for a bus ride home.

Any doubt in my mind about his sincerity, and there were many, was amplified when an acquaintance of his walked by inquiring, as he looked at me, how his business was going. I left him in the cafe and continued my walk around Nairobi wondering how these urchins could identify the new arrivals.

There must be some invisible, universal "kick me" sign that customs agents stick on your back when you land. After a day, it falls off and you are free to travel without bother.

Diving for Shipwreck Treasure: Cue the *Jaws* Theme

How do you get people through the front door of a museum? We discovered – no secret here – that an active schedule of traveling exhibits brings in visitors and grows the ranks of our membership. So we worked continuously to find great traveling exhibits.

When the announcements of new traveling exhibits arrived from national museum associations, I read each with great anticipation. Quickly, I discovered two problems. First, few of the exhibits were enticing. One of my predecessors as museum director had booked a Smithsonian exhibit on needlepoint for a June opening. Florida in the summer is time for families to visit science museums and needlepoint isn't the draw we needed. The Smithsonian curators were horrified when I canceled that exhibit. They said no one had ever cancelled one of their exhibits. We created our own active exhibit and set an attendance record for the summer.

Uninspiring offerings were the first issue. The second issue is often big city museums had reserved the better exhibits before the announcement was released to the rest of the museum world. Several times, I called to book an exhibit the day the announcement arrived only to find that there were no openings left in the tour.

So we took matters into our own hands. I listened to our savvy marketing director and along with the exhibits staff we found exhibit themes that appealed to our audience. One of the topics was treasure and since Florida was the shipwreck treasure capital of the country, we organized several exhibits on treasure.

Luckily for us the most successful treasure diver was a member and supporter of our museum, the South Florida Science Museum. Frogfoot Weller and his wife, Margaret, spent most of their time diving in the shallow waters near Ft. Pierce, Florida. They had gathered a large collection of treasure over the years and were happy to share it for an exhibit. They were also happy to help us recruit other treasure divers to loan their collections.

Frogfoot invited my wife, Barbara, and me to visit him at his home. We were enjoying a relaxed conversation about treasure and diving when he asked if we wanted to see some of his finds.

"Of course," we said.

Frogfoot told us to: "Reach under the sofa you're sitting on and pull out the silver bar."

I had to get down on the floor to wrestle the 80 pound ingot of silver. He pointed out the various markings on the ingot including an assay mark and a tax stamp. He showed some other smaller pieces and described what he could provide for an exhibit. We were hooked. These artifacts told fascinating stories.

Let me point out that Frogfoot was not an underwater archaeologist trying to piece together the history of each wreck he dove on. He was a treasure diver. Most of the artifacts and treasure from each of the ships in this wayward treasure fleet (1715) had been recovered decades or centuries ago. Weller was working in wave tossed, shallow water a few hundred yards from the beach far from the context of the ship that had carried the treasure there. He was looking for the odd bits and pieces that had washed away from the wreck sites and had eluded earlier divers.

Sitting in the Weller's living room, Frogfoot invited Barbara and me to accompany them on a treasure dive. "Yes," we said. We dove recreationally nearly every week off Palm Beach and were very comfortable underwater with SCUBA. Treasure diving would be a new adventure for us.

Frogfoot subleased a site near Ft. Pierce from Mel Fisher, the famed discoverer of the Atocha. The Atocha was a Spanish treasure ship that sank in 1622 off the Florida Keys. It took Fisher 16 years to find the wreck and a few years more to recover $450 million of Atocha's treasure. Fisher started treasure diving in the 1960's and had purchased many of the treasure lease sites from the State of Florida. Mel wanted to move on to more productive locations and so he subleased some sites to other divers.

On the day we dove, Frogfoot anchored his boat, Pandion, in six feet of water a few hundred yards off the beach. He used four anchors to hold the boat steady. His chart of the area showed a black circle at each of the hundreds of locations they had previously explored. After convincing themselves that they had completely searched each square foot of bottom, they would move the Pandion a few feet, re-anchor the boat, and start diving again.

Pandion

Frogfoot and other shallow water treasure divers use the boat's propeller to scour the bottom and reveal treasure and artifacts. With the boat securely anchored, we lowered a large metal device, called a prop wash deflector, over the stern. With the engine running, the propeller pushed water backwards and the deflector directed the stream of water downward, toward the bottom. The stream lifted and swirled sand off the bottom so a diver could search for buried artifacts.

We lay on the bottom underneath the prop wash deflector, drawing our air supply from a compressor on board the boat. We were positioned five or six feet directly beneath the churning propeller. The noise from the engine and prop made it impossible to hear anything else, and the swirling sands limited visibility from a few inches to at most two to three feet. Deaf and nearly blind, we relied on our sense of touch to locate objects in the sand.

The theme from the movie Jaws played in my head, and I wanted to twist around to see what might be lurking behind me, but I couldn't see my own swim fins let alone some imagined monsters a few feet farther away.

The water-borne sand swirled everywhere, and it took days for us to get the sand out of our scalps and ears and from under our fingernails. The positive side of this sand exfoliation was that our skin came out of the water sparkling clean.

Less than an hour after jumping in the water I was cold and tired. Throughout the day I worked until I was uncomfortably cold and then traded places with one of the other three divers. Back on the Pandion we let the warm Florida sun burn the cold from our bodies between dives.

Some treasure divers have experienced the thrill of diving down into clear, warm water, seeing the outline of an ancient ship's hull, and knowing that treasures awaited them. We did not. We found a few Spanish ship artifacts, some broken pieces of pottery. Barbara found a library card. We found no gold, silver, or treasure of any sort. The objects we recovered were not valuable enough to pay for the cost of gasoline for the boat, let alone any wages or profits.

Barbara and I went home that night happy for the experience, but delighted not to be repeating it the next day. Frogfoot and Margaret, however, went back the next day to continue their quest. That day they found several silver coins, including a rare one worth $20,000.

Mel Fisher had a favorite saying: "Today's the day." Today is the day we will find the sunken treasure. If at the end of the day he had not found any treasure he would wait for the sun to rise and repeat, "Today's the day." All treasure hunters must have a similar mantra and faith. Without it they would quickly quit.

Barbara dances with a wunderpus in Lambeh Strait, Indonesia. This is a new species, first scientifically described in 2006.

Sinking a Rolls Royce in the Atlantic Ocean

For nearly a week the national news followed the story of Palm Beach socialite Molly Wilmot. Poor Molly; a derelict freighter, the Mercedes, had washed up on her beach in November 1984 and her life was (temporarily) ruined. It blocked her view of the Atlantic Ocean. Not too many tears were shed for her loss, but the news media fawned over her every day.

It dawned on the diving and fishing community that the freighter could become Palm Beach County's first artificial reef, once it was pulled off Molly's doorstep. As director of the science museum and aquarium, I joined a group to create the artificial reef committee of the county government. I was elected Vice Chair and later Chair when the appointed county councilman enjoyed his afterhours perks of his office a bit too much.

Alas, paperwork takes time and we weren't approved to take the Mercedes by the time a tug yanked it off the beach. Broward County purchased the ship and with the benefit of 350 pounds of explosives added it to their collection of sunken vessels. We were miffed, but pushed ahead with our plans to start an artificial reef program. Soon, a surprising offer was presented to us: "Take my Rolls."

A Palm Beach hairdresser had an old Rolls Royce and offered to donate it to be our first drop in the ocean. Since Broward County got "our" Mercedes, we would upgrade by sinking a Rolls.

93

The County graciously cleaned up the car, removing the engine and fuel tank. From some money that had been donated we hired a tug and barge, and mounted the Rolls on the barge. We were ready to make history.

The barge, with Rolls atop, was anchored just off Palm Beach inlet. Four helicopters circled overhead carrying the national television news crews. Hundreds of private boats surrounded us.

The soon-to-be-displaced county commissioner, the hair dresser, and I stood on the barge. We were dressed in "black tie" although as a concession to my imminent dive, I wore wet suit bottoms, a dress shirt, and black bow tie.

I'm on the left; the donor of the car is standing on the hood; and a Palm Beach county commissioner is walking to the end of the barge. Photo by John Lopinot.

At the appointed time we started pushing on the back of the car. Not much happened until the tug boat took up the slack in the line tied to the front bumper and pulled the car into the Atlantic Ocean. A few bubbles erupted on the sea surface and nice cheers erupted from the assembled throng, signaling that we had our first reef.

The Scuba Club of the Palm Beaches had a dive boat pick me up from the barge and quickly I suited up to dive. A group of us jumped in and finned to the bottom to find the car. It had landed wheels down in perfect position.

For years, divers enjoyed having their photos taken in front of the Rolls. Eventually people pulled off pieces of the car and the rest rusted away. The last time I saw it, only the tires showed out of the sand.

I'm giving the Rolls a final push over the end of the barge. Photo by John Lopinot.

It wasn't much of a fish haven, but it did launch a very successful artificial reef program for Palm Beach

County. Sink a few ships, dump lots of concrete rubble, and marine life settles in to new homes.

I'm on the left in my dress shirt. Norine Rouse, scuba legend, is in yellow grabbing the Spirit of Ecstasy hood ornament.

Years later the Rolls Royce Reef off Palm Beach

Museum Director's Rookie Mistakes

The South Florida Science Museum hired me with
zero experience running a museum. It worked out
well for the institution and for me. I learned so much,
and we advanced the museum, reached new
audiences, and put the museum on solid financial
footing. But along the way I made mistakes.

It was part of the learning process I told myself. Some
of the mistakes I won't mention, but here is one.

The State of Florida loaned us several artifacts for our
several exhibits on shipwreck treasure. For the first
exhibition I had requested some coins, some unusual
artifacts, and three cannon. The state curators
agreed and even sent everything to us in a truck.

I had envisioned they would send a truck with a lift
gate. Or, maybe I didn't envision the problem at all. In
either case a pickup truck arrived from Tallahassee
with the loan material. The guys from the state
museum had been driving for six hours. They wanted
to offload and be on their way home.

They inquired about our forklift. We didn't have a
forklift. "How do you propose to get the three 1,200
pound cannon out of the truck and into the
museum?" they asked.

I didn't know the weight of the cannon and thought
we could man-haul them in. No way.

We spent some minutes at the front door of the
museum thinking of solutions. Meanwhile the state

97

guys were looking at their watches, wanting to get on the road.

I grabbed the Yellow Pages and looked up companies that rented cranes. I learned that it would take hours to get a crane to us and would cost way more than we could afford.

The flash of insight occurred just as the state guys were threatening to haul the cannon back to Tallahassee. I called a tow truck company.

When the driver arrived I explained what we needed to have done. Strap the cannon, lift them one by one out of the pickup truck, back up to the entrance of the museum, and rest the cannon on our pallet jack. The driver was intrigued by all of this and happy to help.

In short order the three cannon were unloaded and safely wheeled into the museum. The state guys were on their way home with an empty truck. The only remaining question was what to pay the driver.

I asked him and he scratched his chin. He confessed that he had never lifted cannon into a museum before so he didn't have experience to base his fee on. I asked what he would have charged to come to the museum and tow a car. "That's easy, $40." He agreed that was a fair price for moving cannon and a lot more fun.

Lassoed by a Shark Sucker

After we opened the South Florida Aquarium at the South Florida Science Museum in West Palm Beach, we needed to re-supply it periodically with specimens. Every few months Palm Beach Atlantic College would loan us one of their yachts (donated for the tax write-off) and a captain, and we would take a handful of volunteer divers and the media to go collecting.

These were wonderful trips. The divers were delighted to help us re-stock our tanks and the television and print media thought it was a great assignment. Who wouldn't want to spend an afternoon diving and taking photos or video underwater on a warm, sunny Florida afternoon? It sure beats covering boring meetings at city hall.

Besides gathering fish and invertebrates, the museum's other goal was to land a photo and story in the Palm Beach Post, Miami Herald, or Sun Sentinel and on the local evening TV news. All three papers reached our potential audience and a nice photo would promote the museum and aquarium, and would bring visitors. So we were delighted to have the diving photographers and reporters accompany us. Our challenge was to give them a new "news" angle so they could convince their assignment editors that they needed to cover each collecting expedition.

Each story or photo that made the news made it more difficult for us to interest the assignment editors for the next collecting trip. They didn't want to send reporters if there was nothing new. We didn't want to hear "We covered that before" from the assignment editors.

To generate news-worthiness for the next collecting trip we had to get more creative.

For some trips we'd explain that we were going after a specific and unusual fish or benthic organisms. For one trip we released a shark from our aquarium that had grown too large for the tanks.

We were stuck for an idea when someone donated a remora, or shark sucker, that was too large for our tanks. This, we decided, was our opportunity. Before releasing it back into the sea, we would use it to help us catch fish. This is an accepted practice in some parts of the world, but as far as we know had never been tried by SCUBA divers.

With some fanfare we announced that we would conduct an experiment to see if we could catch fish using a remora. Remora attach themselves to sharks, rays, fish, and mammals to get free rides. The assignment editors loved the idea and sent a record number of reporters and photographers. We gathered the group aboard the college's boat and headed out through Palm Beach Inlet.

We tied a cloth ring around the peduncle of the remora, the narrowest part of the animal in front of its tail. To that we tied a fishing line spun out from a cheap rod and reel. One of the divers would operate the rod and reel underwater. The hope was that the shark sucker would find a host, attach itself to the host, and our diver could reel in the shark sucker still attached to the host. Then one of the other divers would transfer the captured fish to a holding bag and would release the remora to get more specimens.

The diver holding the rod and reel accompanied me into the water to get into position. I carried a mesh bag with the remora. We waited on the bottom in about 60' of water until the photographers and reporters were hovering above us. Then I released the remora.

Now if you are an experienced SCUBA diver you might see a few potential issues with this experiment. But science pushes on to address questions like these.

Using a hand net to collect fish for the South Florida Aquarium

I had never thought remora were particularly smart, but this one instantly assessed the situation and created a devious escape plan. As soon as I released it, it swam in a circle around us, limited by the fishing line that had been released. As the fishing diver let out more line, the remora swum upward in larger circles. Around and around it swam, rising higher in the water. After two or three passes it was swimming around the photographers and reporters entangling them in the fishing line. In just a few minutes, it had lassoed our group of divers. They were struggling to get free of the fishing line. We had no option but to cut the remora loose.

Fishing with a remora was a complete bust. But, we finished the dive by hand collecting some nice specimens for the aquarium and the news media wrote wonderful stories about the remora that lassoed the divers. The color photos appeared on the front page, local section, above the fold. Nice catch.

King of Treasure Divers

Mel Fisher was King of Treasure Divers. His discovery and recovery of the Atocha treasure (sunk in 1622) returned some $450 million worth of gold, silver, and historic artifacts. He controlled some of the most unique treasure recovered from shipwrecks and so we went to Mel when organizing an exhibit on treasure.

A board member from the South Florida Science Museum had done some business with Mel and arranged our first meeting. He and I flew to Key West and walked into Mel's office. No Mel. Yes, we had an appointment his secretary verified and no, Mel wasn't there. Where was he? No one knew. We flew home chagrined.

Our second attempt was more successful. We were ushered into Mel's office just before noon on a warm summer day. Chaos ruled the office. Every few minutes his secretary interrupted our meeting to announce a phone call. Mel waved her off, declining to take each call, but she would return just a few minutes later with yet another call holding.

"Mel," she announced one time, "you should take this one. He wants to invest." Mel probably made more of his income from investor's money than from directly selling gold doubloons and pieces of eight.

"No," Mel told her. She immediately returned: "Mel, he says he wants to invest $50,000."

"Later," Mel told her. She immediately returned: "Mel, he's serious. He'll put up $100,000." Mel took the call.

We stepped out at noon to get some lunch. We hadn't accomplished anything in our first hour and lunch was no more successful. Everyone in Key West wanted to shout "hi" to Mel Fisher or come over and shake his hand. Mel was beaming. Not only was he King of Treasure Divers, he was also King of Key West. Now ebullient Mel threw down two double shooters over lunch that would have floored me, but he managed to navigate back to his office just fine.

After lunch Mel immediately expressed agreement to our proposal. Yes, he would loan us the artifacts we wanted for the exhibit. Before we could ask what he wanted in return, he told us: half of the admission revenue.

We could not give away half of the admissions. That income paid for salaries and overhead and even with the big crowds of visitors we expected, losing half the revenue would be a financial disaster for the museum. I thought the deal had just fallen apart, but my business- savvy board member spoke up.

"Mel," he said, "we agree to your terms, but you don't want to take money from old ladies do you?"

"No," Mel answered, "I don't want to take money from old people."

You could almost hear our admissions cash register cheer "Ca-ching."

104

"And, Mel, you don't want to take money from kids and school groups do you?"

"Of course not." Mel was obviously a soft touch. "Ka-ching."

"That's great," the board member continued. "We don't charge our members to come in, so there is no gate to split there." Mel couldn't argue with that. "Ka-ching."

In less than a minute Mel had agreed to take a small fraction of the admissions revenue instead of half. The financial success of the exhibit was now assured.

Mel made some money on the exhibit, but not as much as he thought he would. He did insist that we allow his company to set up their own store within the museum. We tried to convince him that it wouldn't be worth the effort and that we could sell his merchandise in the museum store, but he insisted. The first day of the exhibit his store sales topped $13,000. But the next day one person returned a single $12,000 item for refund. A week into the exhibit, Mel closed the store.

We arranged a Mel Fisher Appreciate Day and even officials from the State of Florida, which had been feuding with him for years, attended and said nice things about him. He had taken the State to the US Supreme Court three times over ownership of the artifacts and won. Mel and his wife attended and were truly touched as hundreds of school kids joined us and expressed their appreciation for his discovery of historic shipwrecks. It was a fitting tribute to the King of Treasure Divers.

The exhibit was a grand success.

Many people think ill of Mel for salvaging historic shipwrecks. Some have criticized me for working with Mel.

I liked Mel and respected his tenacity all those years looking for the Atocha. To keep at his quest and pay the terrible cost of losing one son and daughter-in-law, he had to be an optimist. His favorite phrase was: "Today's the day!" meaning that today is the day we will find the mother lode; today's the day of our good luck. And, when today turned out not to be "the day" he would awake the next morning and boldly proclaim: "Today's the day."

Mel was not an archeologist. He didn't dive to learn history. He dove to recover treasure. His tenacity and enduring positive attitude are what I treasured.

Mel Fisher enjoying the Mel Fisher Appreciation Day at the South Florida Science Museum

Transporting Treasure

A few months after meeting Mel Fisher I flew back to
Key West to pick up the artifacts. West Palm Beach
radio station WRMF offered to fly me there in their
traffic reporting airplane. They offered to transport
the treasure and me as long as their morning show
host, Kevin, could accompany me. They'd get
exclusive interviews and some cool stories to talk
about on the morning show. We just had to ensure
that the plane was back in time so it could cover the
afternoon rush hour.

WRMF not only flew me to Key West, they also paid
for the rental car to go from the airport to Treasure
Salvors. We picked up the artifacts – worth some $13
million – and headed back to the airport.

As we drove to the airport I was anxious to get to the
safety of the airplane. Behind every palm tree I
imagined bad guys hiding in wait to grab the treasure.
Kevin was less concerned with security and more
concerned with getting something to eat. He steered
the car to Burger King.

I was frantic. I didn't want to be sitting in the parking
lot of a Burger King and having someone decide to
have it their way with our gold. But Kevin would not
be dissuaded and he held the keys to the car.

I waited and waited in the car with the treasure while
Kevin went inside to place his order. Then I noticed
billows of black smoke pouring out of the Burger King;
it was on fire.

A diversion, I thought. The crooks set fire to the Burger King to divert attention away from the treasure sitting in the back seat of our rental car. Now I was really frantic. I yelled at Kevin to come back to the car, but he held up one finger to indicate that his order was next. Fire or no fire, he was going to get his Whopper.

My anxiety was wasted. We got to the West Palm Beach airport safely with Kevin well fed. Although we had no security in Key West, our landing was protected by two police dogs and a troop of officers from the sheriff's office and police department. All of that for show to the local media. A commercial armored car was there to transport the treasure to the museum. Where were all these guys when I really wanted them?

Dinosaur with a Broken Neck

Animated dinosaurs were the newest thing on the traveling exhibit circuit in the 1980's. Our second exhibit of the moving, bellowing rubber skinned giants was a huge success. And, it just got bigger when the T-Rex broke its neck.

T-Rex was supposed to rotate its head smartly left and right as it opened and shut its jaws to the accompaniment of his tape recorded growl. But after a few weeks on display T-Rex broke his neck. A metal bolt inside its neck snapped and his head hung limp.

Our first reaction was to get this fixed quickly. Wiser heads prevailed however, and we waited for the upcoming holiday. With Thanksgiving only a week away, we opted not to fix it.

Tuesday preceding the holiday we trailered the life-size T-Rex to a hospital near the South Florida Science Museum. It's not easy to take a 10' tall dinosaur for a hospital visit, but our Curator of Exhibits had a personal trailer that we were able to load Mr. Rex onto. The sight of a nearly life-size dinosaur on I-95 drew a few stares.

At the hospital we pushed it into the radiology department where a museum board member who was a radiologist was waiting. Also waiting were about 50 reporters and news photographers. This was a slow news week and the media could not resist the story of an injured dinosaur going to a hospital.

Our radiologist took several X-rays and then shared them with the assembled crowd of journalists. He pointed out the break and suggested how repairs could be done. He played his role perfectly as if he took x-rays of dinosaurs every day.

The story was covered that night on the evening news and the following morning in the daily papers. It was repeated the day after Thanksgiving – the busiest museum day of the year.

That holiday weekend brought crowds of visitors to see the broken neck dinosaur. People would ask the receptionist if they were in the right place to see the dinosaur with a broken neck. They wanted to see the one that had been on television and in the paper.

We decided eventually to repair the broken neck and when we did, our attendance dropped. No one wanted to see the dinosaur that formerly had the broken neck; they wanted to see the real thing, even if the machine didn't work.

Along the Great Wall of China

We were standing in the western Gobi Desert and, aside from sand, nothing was visible. The road had ended miles earlier and we had taken to camels and horses to get here.

Riding a camel is as awkward a form of transportation as any. To get to its feet the camel lurches forward, all but throwing off the unsuspecting rider, then lurches backward to ensure the rider has fallen off. Riding a camel is similar to riding a mechanical bull, but the bull doesn't hate you for riding it.

We had arrived at this empty spot in the desert after a week of driving. Two thousand years ago this had been an oasis frequented by caravans on the Silk Road. Now there was nothing but sand and rocks: no trees, no oasis, and no people.

Our caravan consisted of two cars with two representatives of Gansu Province, a translator, two drivers, an historian and an archaeologist, plus a colleague of mine from Fresno, California.

The official Chinese host knelt down and ran his fingers through the sand. In seconds he found a shard of iron about the size of my thumb nail. He showed it to the two experts and they agreed that it was the iron backing of a mirror that had long ago been dropped and broken at the oasis. It is stunning to think that there are so many bits of debris from centuries ago that he could find an example in seconds.

My hosts had brought us here to get an idea of the environment Silk Road travelers passed through. We had followed the Yellow River out of Lanzhou and then drove westward along a 1,000 km section of the Great Wall to its end. And now starting from where the road ended, we rode camels beyond the end of the Great Wall into the wilderness the caravans had crossed.

I'm riding a camel into the Sand Desert in search of artifacts

For a week we followed the wall along the edge of the Gobi Desert. We visited the remnants of fortresses, watch towers, and towns. Most of the route was empty, but then we would emerge from the desert into a city or state farm.

At one place the road was blocked with a make-shift barricade manned by a dozen workers. They refused to move, blocking our progress. They told us to return the way we had come. There were no alternate routes here. So the lead driver, a husky man, learned that the workers' boss was resting in the only building visible, a tiny shed, on the landscape. The driver walked to the shack and spent a few minutes inside. When he emerged he was holding their boss by one ear and soon we were on our way.

Many of the residents we encountered were fascinated by us, two Americans. Little children either ran away in fear or ran towards us with squeals of delight at seeing something novel. In larger towns film crews followed our every move, but few asked for interviews as they spoke as much English as we spoke Chinese.

As we drove and photographed the Great Wall, we negotiated the arrangements for our exhibition. Gansu Provence wanted to promote tourism and commerce. The Province had paid all our expenses plus expenses for two Central California agricultural businessmen who had accompanied us, but returned home before we began our caravan along the Great Wall.

By the end of the trip we had reached an agreement on the size, scope, contents, and fees. The negotiations were not easy and each time we thought we were making serious progress, something would interrupt the meeting and we would lose the momentum we had achieved. There were many mayors to meet, other officials to pay respects to, and important sites to see. But when we boarded the airplane to fly home, we shook hands and anticipated the major exhibition.

Then nothing. Months went by and our letters (before email) went unanswered. Eventually we learned that another museum had negotiated a major exhibition and had agreed to pay three times the fee we had offered. It appears we were out-bid even though we didn't know someone else was bidding.

No exhibition. But a wonderful experience, my first time in China. Fifteen years later we took one of our exhibitions to China - but that is another story.

Creating the National Toy Hall of Fame

We had already announced our intention to create the US National Toy Hall of Fame. That announcement drew a respectable number of the news media and yielded decent coverage. Now, months later, we were ready to open the toy hall of fame and were worried that the story had already been told. Would the media pay attention?

A. C. Gilbert's Discovery Village was my fifth and last museum directorship. It was a small children's museum, much smaller than the other museums I had led. What attracted me to it was its association with America's greatest toy inventor, A. C. Gilbert.

Gilbert was America's foremost toy inventor and maker throughout the first half of the twentieth century. His toys included my childhood favorites: Erector Set and American Flyer Trains. He had a full line of educational toys like chemistry sets and even a radioactivity set. Really! That didn't stay on the market long. The museum was housed initially in the home of Gilbert's uncle.

Most professional engineers of my generation were Gilbert toy fans. Many tell me that playing with Erector Sets is what got them interested in engineering. I learned the principles of electricity by messing around with my American Flyer trains.

Forty years later I arrived at the museum as it was about to undergo a major expansion. They had raised the funding and hired the designers and contractors and were soon to embark on a "community build."

Much of the labor to build a huge outdoor playground/learning facility was made of volunteers from the community. The plans expanded even more in the months after I arrived.

The museum staff had been 10 dedicated people, all but one had worked there several years. When the board noticed that one-by-one the staff were finding other jobs they discovered that my predecessor was a disaster.

By the time they hired me, only two employees remained on the payroll. One had waited to leave until I came onboard. That left one employee, the bookkeeper, and me. The bookkeeper marched into my new office on day one and demanded that I hire an assistant to help her. Two bookkeepers on a staff of three seemed over-kill. We talked for a few days, but she was adamant and not very good at her job, so I fired her. Now we were down to one employee, me.

As so often happens in nonprofits, miracles occur. Luckily, two volunteers stepped forward to handle the accounting and to help with on-going programs. I quickly hired wonderful staff to fill out the other positions and we lurched forward.

Soon the "build" was upon us. Every day was an adventure expanding A. C. Gilbert's Discovery Village. We continued to seek funding and were successful in getting it, so our building plans grew. Near the end of the build I got the idea for an Oregon Toy Hall of Fame.

A toy hall of fame would appeal both to families and to older people. Salem, home of the Discovery Village, was frequented by busloads of touring seniors. Since our weekday traffic, kids in school groups, disappeared at noon, we could accommodate the bus tourists in the afternoon. And, could there be a better way to honor A. C. Gilbert?

A Portland law firm checked registered trademarks for an Oregon Toy Hall of Fame. The name wasn't registered. On a whim I asked them to check National Toy Hall of Fame. No one had registered that either. I asked them to register the national name.

We had space within the newly expanded A. C. Gilbert's Discovery Village to exhibit toys in the Hall of Fame. We had added several historic buildings to the Village during the build and now had significantly more indoor exhibit space.

To make a hall of fame we needed the toys and a way to select them. I contacted industry and education experts nationwide and we quickly had a distinguished panel of selection judges. Twenty years later that panel of judges still makes the annual selection for the National Toy Hall of Fame.

At this point we released the news to the media. Our hope was the announcement would generate support and interest in planning tours. The media response was solid and public reaction was positive.

A few months later we had our initial inductees identified and were building displays. How could we get the press interested in covering our opening?

117

We thought of all the toys that didn't make it into the first class of inductees. They would be disappointed. Would the toys not selected be disappointed enough to protest?

A college located a few blocks away agreed to recruit students to dress up as disappointed toys. Raggedy Ann had been selected for induction, but Raggedy Andy had not. One student dressed up as Andy and carried a protest sign: "I want in".

There were about two dozen students protesting outside the museum as we started our press conference to open the National Toy Hall of Fame. When we had first announced that we would create the Toy Hall of Fame, one television station sent a crew from Portland to cover the announcement. Now, with the protest march in full swing, four Portland film crews plus print and radio reporters attended.

After I made my statement opening the Hall, I heard one reporter talking on the phone to his assignment editor in Portland. He said: "No. We've got to stay here. They're really protesting outside. This is great."

The press covered the event well, and people around the country and world learned of this new hall of fame. We started with no budget and created an attraction that many people wanted to visit.

The National Toy Hall of Fame opened in Salem, Oregon in 1998. Since then, it has moved and been incorporated into the National Museum of Play in Rochester, New York, where it is expanding annually and doing quite well.

Traveling on a paper rocket

After I left A. C. Gilbert's Discovery Village I launched a tiny business to create and rent exhibits to museums. My real motive was to provide museums with workshops on our philosophy of learning, but few museums had funding for training. Most have funding for traveling exhibits. So we created several exhibits and gave workshops for free to museums that leased our exhibits throughout the US, Norway, Sweden, China and Indonesia.

Later I dropped the exhibits and focused on giving workshops. We've given them now in more than 25 countries.

One of my workshop innovations is a paper rocket launcher. Teachers around the world have seen it and fallen in love with it. So I'm fond of saying: "Paper rockets have transported us around the world."

The Man with a Sub-machine Gun Said: "Give the Nice Policeman Some Money"

He was at least 6' 4" tall and broad in the shoulders. He was a potential tight end in the NFL, except that he was holding a sub-machine gun and blocking my exit from the Lagos airport.

I had traveled to Nigeria to train science teachers. I had never met the people who organized the training, but they were to pick me up at the airport. This is a common arrangement, but usually the host stands outside the customs and immigration exit holding a sign with my name on it. No sign. No host. As I stood in front of the soldier I only hoped they would arrive very soon.

It had been an 18 hour flight and I was tired. The first person I had met after clearing customs and immigration scammed me up for $1. She was standing in front of two armed soldiers and looked official. She asked to see my shot record. Yes, I carry my shot record and could have retrieved it from my backpack, but she offered an easier alternative. She would let me pass for $1. I pulled out one of the few dollar bills in my pocket and gave it to her. All the while I was asking myself if she was an official, but corrupt, inspector or a scam artist with two large friends in the army. Maybe in Nigeria there is no such distinction.

My one dollar toll payment got me past the two soldiers and out the front door of the airport into the sweltering heat that is Nigeria. I took but two more steps when another very big soldier stepped in front of me. This one was the NFL prospect for tight end.

He introduced himself by saying: "Give the nice policeman some money."

In situations like this I become circumspect. The nice policeman had a large sub-machine gun inches in front of my chest and even without the sub-machine gun he was an intimidating figure.

My right hand scrambled back into the nearly empty pants pocket; with fingers digging furiously to find at least a few dollars I might give to my new friend. My fingers didn't find much and I was starting to think of what the consequences might be of disappointing the nice policeman.

Just then, a taxi pulled up behind us. Out jumped a young woman who ran and squeezed herself between the nice policeman and me. She stared into my eyes and said: "Get into the car, Dr. Sobey."

My lips moved in rapid quiver trying to explain that my friend, the police officer, was waiting for financial remuneration. Before I could utter a sensible sentence the young lady said again in a clear and measured tone: "Get into the car….now!"

I did.

As I moved toward the car door I nodded my farewell to the nice policeman and watched to see what he would do, which was nothing. The young lady turned to face him and she had some words with him that I couldn't hear. But, I was in the taxi and the policeman had not moved.

"Welcome to Nigeria," she said as she hopped into the taxi and off we went.

Leroy Just Got Out

Leroy just got out. At first I didn't understand. What does "just got out" mean?

I had been invited to Chicago to train the trainers of a small nonprofit organization. The group hired older kids from poor neighborhoods to be the counselors and teachers for summer programs. They had affiliated themselves with *Kids Invent!* (a company I helped create) and I was there to help them launch science-based summer programs.

The local group was responsible for providing my lodging and ground transportation. A week before the trip they let me know that there were no hotel rooms available in all of Chicago. Really? A huge conference, they told me, was coming to town. Would I mind staying at the home of the board president?

Knowing that there are some very nice homes in Chicago and that presidents of nonprofit boards often live in such homes suggested that the switch from a hotel to private residence could be nice. But now, as the board president was driving me from the airport through the slums of south Chicago I was reconsidering.

Each side street we passed was more dilapidated than the preceding one. As we came upon each new city block I prayed to myself: "Please don't turn down this street." I was hoping we would suddenly emerge onto an urban oasis. Instead, when we got to the worst street I had seen, we turned and he parked his car.

122

As we walked up to the house in greatest disrepair on this, the worst street I had seen, the board president apologized. Even though it was the middle of the summer and was uncomfortably hot he informed me that "All the downstairs windows are screwed shut - to keep out the druggies and gang bangers." He went on to say that there was one air conditioner in the house, but it was mounted in a second floor window and I would be staying on the first floor.

He took me into a room. My room. The only thing in the room was a mattress lying on the floor and a pillow. No bed. No other furniture. Nothing but the mattress and pillow. My expectations shattered, I was trying to find some silver lining and kept coming up short.

A few minutes later the board president told me he had to go pick up Leroy. Leroy would be staying with me this week in the adjoining room. The board president would be leaving in two days for an out-of-town meeting, but Leroy was moving in and he knew Chicago so he would help me during the week. As he walked out the door, he added that "Leroy just got out."

My mind raced to find the question I could ask to help me understand. Before he reached the sidewalk I blurted out: "How long has Leroy been in?" I was hoping for something short - a few days for neglecting to pay parking tickets or some such thing.

"He's been in for 17 years. Armed robbery."

123

He drove off to pick up Leroy leaving me to contemplate my options. I could call a cab and head back to the airport, but I would lose my pay for the week and the airfare. I could start calling hotels and hope I could find a room. Or, I could put off a decision and see if and how I survived the first night.

I procrastinated, which is to say, I was unable to take decisive action.

It turns out that Leroy was a model house-mate. Yes, he had been "in" for 17 years and he never wanted to go back "in" again. Leroy wanted to be helpful. No, he needed to be helpful. So he grabbed my bag of tools each morning and evening and carried it for me between the house and the nonprofit. He kept asking me if he could do something for me or get something for me. Leroy was a gem.

I survived the week. It was not the week I had expected or wanted, but it did provide me with an experience unlike any other.

Short hikes

Inside the Volcano

Fog delayed our departure. By 11 AM the helicopter had landed to pick us up and carry us into the caldera of Mt. St. Helens.

The mountain had famously blown its top 32 years before, losing 1,318' of height. By now glaciers had formed inside the caldera and inside some of those rivers of ice were caves. We were flying in to explore those ice caves.

Charlie Anderson was the dean of Cascade Mountain Ice Caves. He had explored and measured them all over many years. His life was devoted to them and he lost his wife in an accident inside one. When he invited me to accompany him I accepted immediately.

Charlie had just given a presentation to the Pacific Northwest Chapter of The Explorers Club. He was a member and I was the chairman of the chapter. After his presentation I pressed him on details of how someone could get into the ice caves. Later his invitation arrived.

I sat in the front seat of the helicopter to the right of the pilot. The flight into the mountain was exhilarating as we flew low over the hillsides and valleys. We landed inside the caldera, about half a mile from the lava dome where the mountain was growing again. Mt. St. Helens had lost 1,000 m of its height to the eruption in May 1980 and now was regrowing inside the caldera.

We dropped off our packs and headed up hill towards the glaciers. We didn't get far before we noticed landslides coming down the inside of the caldera. As we pushed onward and upward the frequency of the landslides increased. Some big chunks of rocks were tumbling hundreds of feet down the inside walls of the volcano. When one microwave-sized rock spun down toward us, seemingly altering its trajectory to match our attempts to avoid it, we decided to stop climbing. Our late start had meant that the daily thawing of ice had started. We could expect an increasing rate of landslides as the ice holding rocks in place melted.

We turned around and headed back to our packs and what would be our overnight campsite. Exploring the floor of the caldera revealed volcanic bombs and tiny piles of sand spaced with consistent spacing on the volcano floor.

There were several streams of hot water rising up out of the floor. Rainwater that had seeped down into the caldera had been warmed by the hot rocks beneath and had re-emerged as springs. The water was too hot to touch where it issued from the ground, but 150m downstream it had cooled enough to be comfortably warm.

Charlie Anderson grabs the last pack out of the helicopter inside
the caldera

Following a stream showed drastic color changes.
Rich growths of brightly colored algae grew in some
places and not in others.

Riffles where the stream dropped a few inches
harbored an astonishing site. Caught in the vortex of
circulating water beneath the several inch water fall
were pearls. I reached down and pulled out half a
dozen.

They weren't smooth oyster-made pearls. Instead
they were roughly shaped and pitted lumps of white
calcite.

127

Stream pearls from inside Mt. St. Helens

After the rain water was heated in the volcano it dissolved minerals. These minerals precipitate out as the water cooled on the volcano floor. At the mini water falls, precipitates aggregated together to form these tumbling pearls.

As the mountain grows the flow of water changes and some streams grow and others die. The pearls I picked up are from a stream that no longer exists. They provide a snapshot of conditions that summer.

We spent one night inside the volcano. Each minor quake of the mountain woke me up. The next morning the helicopter returned to fetch us.

No glacial caves. But stream pearls are pretty cool, too.

Goat Rocks

Six of our family did a backpacking trip into the Goat Rocks Wilderness in Washington State. The day going in was beautiful with blue skies and wildflowers carpeting the hillsides. Hot and tired, we found a nice camping spot near the top of Goat Peak and set up for the night.

Woody and Andrew slept in bivouac bags. Barbara and I sent up our dome tent and Jean and John had their small pup tent.

About midnight, lightning and thunder interrupted our sleep. We listened as the levels of sound and lightning increased. The wind picked up, rocking our tent. The frequency of lightning strikes sped up.

Every lightning strike would start my internal stopwatch counting seconds until thunder roared. Five seconds separation means the lightning is a mile away and not much to worry about. But the separation was getting much shorter.

As wind speed continued to pick up, the lag between the lightning and thunder dropped to less than half a second. The lightning was striking ground less than 500' away. The electric gods were casting bolts of lightning on top of us. One right after another.

I wanted to run to the others to check them, but the strikes were so close I knew I would be struck if I stood up outside. Our voices yelling to the others were lost in the roar of the wind and nearly continuous thunder.

Woody and Andrew, inside their bivouac bags were as close to the ground as possible. Jean and John's tent stuck above the flat landscape. It was supported by aluminum poles; they were like lightning rods sticking above the ground.

Jean yelled: "Take down the poles," letting the tent collapse on top of her and John. Amidst furious rain, water started leaking through their tent.

After a few minutes inside the suffocating collapsed tent, John recognized that they had to open the tent for air circulation. Jean and John tried to decide which the greater danger was: running out of oxygen to breathe or getting hit by lightning.

They decided the lightning was worse and spent the hours of the night gasping for air, trying to stay above the water pooling on the tent floor. After the lightning passed, John put the poles back into the tent.

In our dome tent I thought of going outside to remove our fiberglass poles. The risk of being struck was too great. So we lay awake inside waiting for whatever was to come.

It was the most frightening night we have experienced outdoors. We were in the wilderness, in danger, and unable to improve our situation. We had to ride it out.

The storm persisted for an hour as we huddled in our tents. Hail followed the lightning and littered the ground. When I emerged from our tent in the morning I saw Woody and Andrew's bivouac bags covered with hail.

Jean arose and surveyed the scene. To our relief she found that our backpacks had not blown away in the night.

When we got back to the ranger station we sought out the ranger who had recommended this camping spot. We described our experience with the lightning storm. He chuckled: "Yeah, that mountain is renowned for its lightning."

Bears Ate My Breakfast

The first bear marched into our campsite around midnight. Carl, one of the other scout leaders, nudged me to make sure I was awake.

"There's a bear trying to get our food," he whispered.

"So what," I said. "Dumb bear! He won't get it."

We were leading a group of Boy Scouts on a 50 mile backpack trip in Yosemite National Park. My sons, Woody and Andrew, were among the dozen scouts. This was our last night: tomorrow would be a hamburger and milk shake day after a 6 mile hike out.

The boys had done well. Some were pretty slow hiking with backpacks ten plus miles a day, but they were all game. One of the other fathers had gotten altitude sickness, but seemed now to be over it.

That last night we knew there would be bears nearby so we were especially careful in how we "bear-bagged" our food.

We split the food up into two sets of bags, each to be hoisted in different trees. We found limbs high enough that a bear couldn't reach bags from the ground and small enough not to support the weight of a bear. There was no way a bear could steal our food short of stealing one of our Swiss Army knives and cutting the rope.

Carl suggested that since I was the leader I should get out of the tent and scare the bear away. That was not

132

going to happen. So we both peaked out through our tent to watch the bear's attempt at theft.

He clambered quickly up the tree and out onto the base of the limb. As he started down the limb, it sagged under his weight. He knew the branch wouldn't support him.

At this point I professed how dumb the bear was. Now I could go back to sleep.

But the bear didn't give up. He innovated. He started chewing through the small branch. Each resounding "crunch" announced a bite out of the branch. With each bite, the branch sagged lower.

When the branch was low enough that the food bags touched the ground, the wise Mr. Bear scampered down the tree, snapped the bags, and ran into the darkness.

"Wow," I thought. That's cheating. We did the bear bag picture perfect and he defeated it.

After the adrenalin settled down I tried to get back to sleep. My attempt was soon interrupted by mama bear and two cubs.

Mama was eyeing our other stash of food, high in an adjacent tree. She called a family meeting at the base of the tree as we watched from the tents.

Up the tree climbed the two cubs while mama supervised from the ground. Slowly they made their way to the limb and out to rope holding the bags.

133

They were unsure of themselves now some 15' in the air, but mama was coaching them.

One of the cubs gnawed through the parachute cord holding the bags. In seconds the cluster of food bags, our last food, flopped to the forest floor.

In a flash mama pick up two of the bags and ran out of our campsite leaving the two cubs in the tree. Slowly they made their way down to the ground and took off after her.

They had left one small food bag. Its sole contents were a few granola bars.

Thoroughly defeated in our attempt to protect our food, we spent the rest of the night huddled around our campfire protecting our meager rations.

No more bears visited us that night. The word must have spread throughout the bear world that the robbers had plundered all the treasure.

We broke camp quickly and made record speed over the final few miles marching on empty stomachs. Those bears are pretty smart.

Parting Thought

Fortune has shined on me throughout my life and has allowed me to enjoy exotic experiences and adventures. Many more talented people have stood on the sidelines watching me do cool stuff telling themselves that they couldn't.

Opportunities are out there waiting for you to grab them. For every one you're able to grab you have to invest in nine others that don't pan out. If you're afraid of failing, you won't make that investment.

Here is my suggestion for a compass to guide your life of adventure:

- Stay curious
- Keep exploring; keep creating
- Fail often; fail quickly
- Be persistent, not patient
- Skip the mundane; do cool stuff

Appendix

The Course Navigated

- Valley Forge Military Academy – high school
- University of Richmond, BS in physics and math
- Oregon State University, MS and PhD in oceanography
- US Navy Officer Candidate School
- USNS Michelson T-AGS 3, Oceanographic Unit 3
- Naval Facility Pacific Beach, Washington, Operations Officer
- SAIC – Boulder Office, Environmental Sciences
- South Florida Science Museum, Executive Director
- Jacksonville Museum of Science and History, Executive Director
- National Invention Center and National Inventors Hall of Fame, Executive Director
- Ohio Public Television, Co-host *Blow the Roof Off*
- Fresno Metropolitan Museum, Executive Director
- California State University, Fresno Adjunct Faculty, Assistant to Dean Natural Sciences
- KFSN TV, Executive Producer and Host, *The Idea Factory*
- A C Gilbert's Discover Village, Executive Director
- National Toy Hall of Fame, Founder
- Northwest Invention Center, President
- Pacific Northwest Chapter, The Explorers Club, President
- Northwest Explorers, President

Expeditions

- Northeast Pacific Ocean, Oregon State University (5 research expeditions)
- Oceanographic Unit Three, US Navy, Western Pacific Ocean (10 research expeditions)
- Winter Ice Hole Project, Antarctica, Oregon State University
- El Nino Expedition, Southeast Pacific Ocean, Oregon State University
- Sea Otter Census by Kayak, Southeast Alaska, Expedition Training Institute
- Gray Whale Vocalizations, Southeast Alaska
- Humpback Whale Vocalizations, Southeast Alaska
- Archaeology Survey, Southeast Alaska
- Egypt and Kenya Exhibition Quests
- Inca Exhibit Quest, Peru
- Great Wall of China Exhibition Quest
- Coral Reef Health Survey, University of Belize, The Explorers Club
- Coral Reef Healthy Sounds, Curacao Research State, The Explorers Club
- Trans-Pacific Sail, Tokyo to Seattle

Fellow, The Explorers Club

Fulbright Grants

- Arctic Sweden Professional Development for Teachers
- Indonesia Professional Development for Teachers
- Bhutan Professional Development for Teachers

137

Barbara and Ed at Tiger's Nest, 2019.
Photo by Pelden Dorji Dadil Jamtsho

Training Workshops Given

- Austria
- Sweden
- Norway
- Estonia
- Germany
- Turkey
- Indonesia
- India
- Sri Lanka
- China
- Singapore
- Malaysia
- Bhutan
- Myanmar
- Mexico
- Canada
- Nigeria
- Australia
- Switzerland
- Jordan
- Iceland
- Saudi Arabia
- United Arab Emirates
- Barbados
- St. Vincent
- St. Lucia
- Trinidad and Tobago
- United States

Lecturer at Sea

- Some 33 voyages aboard commercial cruise ships
- Four semesters teaching, Semester at Sea

Jumping into the Arctic Ocean near Iceland

Books Published

- *The Field Guide to Ocean Voyaging: Animals, Ships, and Weather at Sea,* 2018
- *Robotics Engineering* – Learn it, Try it, 2018
- *Electrical Engineering* – Learn it, Try it, 2018
- *Build your own robot – Science Fair Project,* 2015
- *Car Models that Zoom – Creativity in Motion,* 2013 (Translated into Chinese, Turkish, and German)
- *Motor Boat Science – Hands-on Marine Science,* Chicago Review Press, 2013
- *Electric Motor Experiments,* Enslow Publishers, 2011
- *Solar Cells and Renewable Energy Experiments,* Enslow Publishers, 2011
- *Robot Experiments,* Enslow Publishers, 2011
- *Unscrewed: Freeing Motors, Gears, Switches, Speakers, and More from Your Old Electronics,* Chicago Review Press, 2011
- *Radio-Controlled Car Experiments,* Enslow Publishers, 2011
- *The Way Kitchens Work,* 2010
- *A Field Guide to Automotive Technology,* 2009
- *The Way Toys Work,* 2008
- *A Field Guide to Household Technology,* 2007
- *A Field Guide to Office Technology,* 2007
- *A Field Guide to Roadside Technology,* 2006.
- *Rocket-powered Science.* Good Year Books, 2006
- *Loco-Motion: Physics Models for the Classroom.* Zephyr, 2005
- *How to build an award-winning robot,* Enslow, 2002
- *Inventing Toys: Kids having fun while learning science,* Zephyr Press, 2001
- *Fantastic Flying Fun with Science,* McGraw-Hill, 2000
- *Wacky Water Fun with Science,* McGraw-Hill, 2000

- *Young Inventors at Work*, Good Year Books, 1999
- *How to enter and win Invention Contests*, Enslow Publication, 1999
- *The Whole Backpackers Catalog*, Ragged Mountain Press, 1998
- *Just Plane Smart*, McGraw-Hill, 1998
- *Car Smarts: Activities for the Open Road*, McGraw-Hill, 1997
- *Wrapper Rockets and Trombone Straws: Science at Every Meal*, McGraw-Hill, 1996
- *Inventing Stuff*, Dale Seymour Publications, 1995
- *Runner's World Aerobic Weight Training Book,* 1982
- *Runner's World Strength Training Book*, 1981
- *The Complete Circuit Training Guide*, 1980

Canoeing and Kayaking Adventures

Suwanee River
St. John's River
Everglades
Okefenokee
The Peace River
Yellowstone
Upper Missouri
Lower Columbia
The Platte River
Willamette River
Assateague Island
Cache la Poudre

San Juan Islands
Santiam River
Sandy River
The Broken Group
Nootka Sound
Checleset Bay
San Joaquin
Killarney Provincial Park
Temagami River Provincial Park
Bowron Lakes Provincial Park
Southeast Alaska

Backpacking Adventures

Olympic National Park
Mt. Hood
Rocky Mountain National P.
Yosemite National Park
Pinnacles National Park
North Cascades National P.
Goat Rocks Wilderness

Mt. Rainier
Mt. St. Helens
Allegheny National Forest
Sierra National Forest
Alpine Lakes Wilderness
Three Sisters Wilderness

SCUBA and Snorkeling Adventures

South Florida
Bonaire
Curacao
Belize
Honduras
Tobago
Grenada
Cozumel
Bali
Palau
Rangiroa
Fakarava
Ecuador
Galapagos
Red Sea
Bequia
Moorea

Andros Island
Bimini
Eleuthera
Exumas
Turks and Cacaos
Great Barrier Reef
Lambeh Strait
Ambon Island
St. Vincent
St. Lucia
Barbados
Hawaii
Croatia
Oman
Baja
Bora Bora

On the set for the televised science and inventing show, *The Idea Factory,* KFSN-ABC, Fresno. I was the Executive Producer and host.

CPSIA information can be obtained
at www.ICGtesting.com
Printed in the USA
BVHW010434010820
585157BV00001B/11

9 780578 709833